YOU MUST BE KIDDING

Dr.SUPRATIC GUPTA

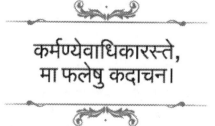

कर्मण्येवाधिकारस्ते,
मा फलेषु कदाचन।

Supratic Gupta
&
Prakash Chandra

ISBN: Hardcover   978-1-4828-4821-2
               Softcover   978-1-4828-4820-5
               eBook   978-1-4828-4819-9

To order additional copies of this book, contact
Partridge India
000 800 10062 62
orders.india@partridgepublishing.com

www.partridgepublishing.com/india

DEDICATION

This book would not have been possible without sharing an awesome and eventful life with wife Rupa and son Sagar.

I would like to express my gratitude from the bottom of the heart to my both Life Co-travellers.

Life would not have been so kind to this crazy man, without either of you.

- Supratic Gupta

Acknowledgements

No creation in this world is a solo effort and both authors are extremely thankful to motivating people, who contributed in completion of this book, right from inception to the final editing stage. They were important part of the awesome caravan of ideas, which we rolled.

Our sincere thanks to Ms. Divya Singh, who designed the book graphics and outlay. Her efforts helped us a lot in completing the book in the present form. We would also like to thank Mr. Kaushal Mahaseth for his contribution in the initial documentation stage of the book.

We are also thankful to our family members, including our life partners, Rupa and Uma, who were pillars of support during the hectic schedule, extending over more than two years. Our children brigade, Sagar, Apoorva and Atharva were constant sources of many inspiring and fresh ideas, particularly in the fields of education, sports, and child rearing. Thanks kids, you were our first school of Hard-Knock Learning! We are grateful to our parents for their blessings. Special thanks are due to Dr. Gupta's brother Prithwish Kumar Gupta and his wife Sara Ann, Sister-in-law Sanchita Gupta and his class mates of 1984 Batch, Ramkrishna Mission Vidyapith, Deoghar, for their support. We are also thankful to Prof. K. S. Rao, Prof. Gurmail Benipal, Prof. K. Ramachandra Rao, Prof. A.K. Nema, Prof. Rakesh Khosa and others at IIT Delhi for their support.

We also extend our sincere thanks to Partridge publications.

Supratic Gupta

Prakash Chandra

Foreword

I remember Supratic when he was a student in Ramakrishna Mission Vidyapith, Deoghar, during the years from 1977 to 1984. I was then serving as Secretary of the Vidyapith. He would often ask strange questions about God, faith and world. For most of his classmates, he was their little maths teacher. I was very happy when Supratic, with his sincere efforts got admission into IIT Madras after securing a good rank in the entrance test.

This book is a compilation of his thoughts based on his professional experience in India and Japan. It is good that Supratic has teamed up with his schoolmate Prakash Chandra, a social worker by profession, to compile their constructive thoughts in the form of book. It is a matter of satisfaction that alumni of our school are coming forward in conceptualizing and penning down their life experiences for the good of others.

I wish both of my students success in their projects and lives. May Sri Ramakrishna, Sri Sarada Devi and Swami Vivekananda ever bless them.

Swami Suhitananda
General Secretary
Ramakrishna Math & Ramakrishna Mission
Belur Math
Howrah, West Bengal - 711202

Table of Contents

The Prologue

The caravan of Dr. Supratic Gupta's rainbow-ideas was assembled in the frantic life storms of Guwahati, Japan and Delhi. Just 4 years back, life's grey undercurrent was rocking his soul-boat like a tossing leaf and he was trying to save his own existence, as well as his wits, around the topsy-turvy world. He had not intended kidding, when he started to pen-down his experiences as well as pains. It started with scores of e-mails, posted randomly to sympathetic ears of a counsellor-cum-friend and co-author of this book Mr. Prakash Chandra. Dr. Gupta was quite serious about important things in life; which seemed too important to be left solely to the discretion of the experts. It is about the life, its ups & downs and the way we look at it; usually in a drab colour, without any enjoyment and entertainment.

A swarm of questions started to haunt him like storms of tormenting thoughts. When he tried to find out some answers, many friends and well-wishers nodded in confusion and asked him politely that if he was kidding? After all, a Professor of prestigious Indian Institute of Technology is supposed to stick to his engineering academic agenda and not sermonize on complex psycho-social issues, without any expert's relevant degrees and credentials. Ignorance to the theoretical knowledge of a complex problem was a mixed-blessing, since it is devoid of any earlier academic influence and bias. The Professor represents the "Aam Aadmi" or a common man's concern on several burning problems.

He wondered why the emergence of India, as a major force in world economy and geopolitical entity is lopsided and full of anomalies, with such gaps, contrasts and holes in the success story of development. Why other Asian countries like Japan, China and Korea have forged far ahead in development, cultural refinement and scientific temper, while India is still in nascent stage of development? Why India has such glaring income and class disparity ranging from low income classes to the so called High Values Assets people? It is important for us, the people of India, to sit down and think - what is important in life and what is lacking in our attitude and values that we have to unlearn and change.

To understand the depth and feeling of the concepts elaborated in the book, it is important to understand the background of Dr. Gupta. He was born in Guwahati, Assam, where his family had settled after migrating from Bangladesh and overcoming a hand-to- mouth existence. With hard work and long hours of tireless efforts, his family soon transformed into a well-off construction company. Inspite of losing his mother in childhood, he grew up in a loving atmosphere of the joint family. He was very intelligent and became a loving child respectful to all in this positive atmosphere. He nurtured into an open- hearted innocent and carefree boy, with an insatiable curiosity of asking too many questions about life, god, untouchability, superstitions, etc. He was a chirpy Pied-Piper, who was apt in winning hearts of all around him. His grandmother used to read to him the books of Ramayana and Mahabharata, which had a major influence on him.

The author and his elder brother grew up in a holistic and nurturing atmosphere of a boarding school, Ramkrishna Mission Vidyapith, situated in Deoghar, Jharkhand. In the school, the stories of Swami Vivekananda and Lord Buddha had a deep impact on his fertile mind. He believed in the concept of "**Karma is Dharma**", with the dictum that one should do his duty sincerely and accept unconditionally the results that follows; good or bad has to be accepted based on a verse from Bhagwad Gita- *Karmanye vaadhikaraste, Maa faleshu kadachana*. Introspection is important, however excessive happiness or regret is harmful. This philosophy helped him to cross difficult stages of his life; as the sad moments to him appeared as mere results of his action.

His life turned out more like the child of the hindi movie 'Tare Jamin Pe', who struggled in almost all subjects in his studies, but was the considered as the best student in mathematics. From his very childhood, he was good in logic and was far ahead in maths in his class, almost by two years. It made him the natural teacher to all of his friends in this subject. Little did the school and friends realize that he was suffering from Attention Deficit Hyperactive Disorder-ADHD, with alternating flashes of brilliance and lethargy. He became serious in study only after Class IX and his dedicated efforts culminated in his getting JEE 326 rank at national level. Despite his high rank, he did not opt for popular engineering streams like Computers Science and joined Civil Engineering in IIT, Madras, by choice. He completed Bachelor's degree from IIT Madras and went to Japan for higher studies, where he spent twelve years, completing his masters and doctoral studies. More importantly, in Japan, he received the opportunity to meet students from all across the world, representing all region and culture, which provided him a deep insight of life.

He was exposed to the inspiring thoughts of Swami Vivekanada and Lord Buddha from the very early childhood. He was fascinated by his grandmother, who narrated to him the mystic Hindu religious and mythological stories. Most of the concepts in book have originated from multi-events and experiences, including those from 12 years of eventful life in Japan, where he had seen the beauty of Japanese society with all its sincerity. His marriage at the age of 24 years, birth of his son after 8 years and the way Japanese society takes care of child birth; all such experiences moved him. Later, the pangs of seeing the shattered dreams of his son of becoming an Olympic level swimmer, inspite of his sincere attempts, raised many questions about the prevailing Indian educational system. He went in depth by going through books on diverse religions and philosophies and travelled worldwide, with similar questions swirling in his mind.

Like a magnet, Dr. Gupta attracted like-minded people and organised a team to give further momentum to his ideas. The co-author of this book, Prakash Chandra joined him three years back as a counsellor and a friend. He was impressed by Dr. Gupta's herculean efforts in organising his concepts as well as his own troubled life and later joined the core content development team. Mr. Prakash Chandra had two decades of experiences in the field of social developmental sector and psychological counselling, while working with leading National and International organizations, including SOS Children's Villages of India (Orphan Care), Nidan and Jaipur Rugs Foundation. A chanced interaction on social media attracted him towards the offbeat and creative ideas of Dr. Gupta. Later, Prakash Chandra, was much impressed by Professor's strong character and passion.

Despite the fact that Dr. Gupta was fighting bravely the battles of his own life with shattered dreams, problematic son (also diagnosed as ADHD) and troubled family; he was still trying to convert the experiences into strength. He was attempting to make effective change in the system through his path-breaking new concepts, with almost a strange aura of smile. As he underwent **Counselling** by Prakash Chandra to overcome his problems, he realised the importance of learning anger control techniques from early stage of life. He realized the importance and significance of providing organized counselling to people of all ages, especially in teens and middle aged, so that they can face expected problems in an organized manner as most of the problem faced by people have set patterns.

For the co-author Prakash Chandra and other group members associated with Dr. Gupta, it was not an easy task dealing with the eccentric Professor. From the very beginning, the concepts were not clear and group struggled for two years to document and give a final shape to this book. To the Professor, it might be a continuous, evolving, stable and logical thought process, but the group found it extremely difficult, to understand and switch between various out-of-box concepts, that he elaborated and presented.

The starting point of the formation of the group coincided with the time, when he was in the process of painfully abandoning the joint dreams of himself and his son, to become an Olympian swimmer. This happened due to lack of support and scientific inputs from the educational and sports system. He was also undergoing adjustment and personal problems at the same time. He spent much time in understanding the life of various sports people and realized the need for science and technology to support the children dedicated to sports, in achieving excellence and entertainment.

He continued to wonder about the fundamental changes in attitude and values that Indian society required. He soon realized that fitness and health are prime issues. One needs a holistic approach to physical health through mass music, dance and exercise and integrate it with entertainment factor. In search of happiness and truth, he wandered from drum circle to Latin dance classes, trying to learn song and dance. For the first time in life, he realized the amalgamation of beats, dance moves and exercise through the lessons of Jumba class. He realized the importance of mass **Music and Dance** in the happiness index of life. He also felt that this **Music and Dance for Street Children** possibly can solve this problem from the route, if we try to empower them and make them earn through entertainment.

He realized that the present education system provides a very unfair situation to the sports-children and this is true for children pursuing music and dance too. As a result, one can see that most successful people like Tendulkar, Kapil Dev, Deepika Padukone, Amir Khan or Abhishek Bacchan concentrated in physical-mental development and building their own career capabilities and requirements from childhood.

This lead Dr. Gupta to realize that these children of special world need a complete separate education system called "Entertainment Stream", where children can spend dedicated hours in childhood to develop their talents, in a happy and satisfying way. Customized courses and teaching modules of science, maths, communication skills etc. can be taught to these children in a **Flexible Education** system, such that they can become complete entertainers for the society. In this entertainment stream, every individual should learn to become a complete entertainer; a balanced personality, who is physically and mentally fit, enjoying all the things and basic skills in life. A sports man would need to learn, how to speak, sing and dance to entertain people in field as well as off the field. This will help him to become more popular, for instance, just like some entertaining performances by the player in world cup football matches, after scoring goals. This will also take care of post-retirement problems of the sportsmen, which is a universal problem. The sportsman can start his post-retirement career as second innings with wide range of possibilities and self-confidence.

For normal children, he proposed the selection of streams from class VIII in place of present system of class X, so that children can have more time to rethink and change lines. He realized the need for creation of a public supported **Education Portal** where all information of different trades would be available so that children can take more informed decision of careers in life.

The sports loving children, willing to dedicate their life to be sports, are also facing severe problems of scientific guidance and lack of modern technology as they are not individually affordable. They also face lack of good coaching as most coaches would like to enjoy the luxury of city life. Hence, the reader supported **Sports Portal** concept would help them bridge the gap.

Changing subjects to **Life of women and Happiness**, he realized that most of the problem in life starts with the unfair deal that women get in life as they have no choice but to become mother and take care of the child. Every effort to create an equal and just society stumbles on her motherhood role. After struggling hard in studies and then pursuing professional career courses; they are put in a dilemma about the quality of upbringing of the child, in case they join a job. The motherhood itself is a great stress-producer. Without proper scientific guidance their relationship with husband also starts suffering. For example, after coming back from Japan, Mrs. Gupta had a dream to open a Bakery. Dr. Gupta had to ignore her dream as the child's dream of being an Olympian swimmer also required time and service of the mother. All these problems can be taken care if we can create good system of childcare in line of **Hoikuen** system of Japan, where child is looked after by trained people, providing a holistic development of 5 senses through gardening, **Swimming and Flexibility Exercise**. We possibly also require a community food system in lines of Shokudo as explained in the book.

While discussing the approach to face life, he shared that people should understand *Scientific Thinking* techniques where one has to have a clear objective for each his actions, such that his conclusions of today's action guide him to a better tomorrow. He also explained that most people can answer questions after reading a text, but what distinguishes an analytical person from others is his ability to write articulately about events or phenomena of life with clear objective. He feels that teaching the techniques and methodology of writing a doctoral thesis along with presentation skills would also help a normal person be an acceptable writer and presenter (**Structure of Research Work**).

While talking about a *public-driven system*, he conceptualized of **Research Portal** fuelled, guided and controlled by public for creating a better **Research Environment in India**. The book also discussed the concept of an ideal **Old Age Home**. He once had visited an old age home in Vridndavan for widow. He proposed that older people should stay in the old age home, where best medical facilities can be provided and they can lead a happy life. They can also help the youth in taking care of their children and establish a type of family relationship on a paid basis, to lead a socially responsible happy life.

The co-author Prakash Chandra would like to request the readers to understand this book as a compilation of serious thoughts of a crazy professor. The concepts are extremely thought provoking. It may sound strange in first reading, but the reader will not be able to ignore the novelty of the approach and may think about the topics/concepts again and again. It is suggested that each chapter be read and re-read independently. This book has a great potential to create a positive wave of change in the world, so that our children can have an enjoyable life with a physically strong and healthy body with clear objective in life. The group led by Dr. Gupta would propose to initiate a few pilot projects to demonstrate these concepts. This group would partner and relate with bodies to participate in implementing these concepts. Most importantly, the authors expect to disseminate these innovative ideas among the public, in a participatory mode, involving them in a greater ways at every stage.

**Flexible
Education**

CHAPTER 1
FLEXIBLE EDUCATION

1.1   Introduction

The Indian Education system carries even today the colonial burden of Macaulay's "Clerk-making Education" formulated in 1835. Even after more than 180 years, it is really pathetic to see the young generation running after degrees, diplomas and secured jobs in a rigid education system, which suppresses creativity. In comparison to other countries, Indian education system is putting undue emphasis on formal education. This disturbs development of skills in other fields of business, music, dance, sports, etc., which has much larger social need and future scope. The existing system is creating great stress on the young students. The author had himself been compelled to watch hopelessly, the tyranny of the rigid education system, washing away of the hope of his son, who just wanted to pursue his dreams of becoming an Olympian swimmer. The story of the shattered dreams of his son compelled the author to think of an alternative flexible education system, which nurtures such dreams and make it more integrated, holistic and sustainable.

> *Indian education system is putting undue emphasis on formal education and this disturbs development of skills in other fields of business, music, dance, sports, etc.*

> *... it is really pathetic to see the young generation running after degrees, diplomas and secured jobs in a rigid education system, which suppresses creativity.*

The author, after coming back to India from Japan, had the opportunity to see the sports world's inner dynamics, through his son's efforts to balance it with the school's academic demand. There was a time, when his son, aged 9 years, shared a dream with him, to become an Olympian in the field of swimming and get selected for 2016 Olympics, when he would be 16 years old. In this process, his son put maximum effort through rigorous training; while the author studied international literature about training techniques, latest technology, food and sleep related details, necessary to achieve excellence for the purpose.

Apart from **lack of infrastructure**, the demand of the rigid study curriculum in school was a great problem, as no relaxation was provided to the child in the form of flexible education system. The school's curriculum was not flexible enough to give some space to the aspiring child, while the professional coaches were not prepared to adapt to new coaching techniques.

The author and his son had to abandon their dreams. The level of educational flexibility and existence of international technology may vary across India, but it is far from ideal. Even though the author gave up the dream of his son to become an Olympic swimmer, he is still continuing his effort and proposed a flexible education system.

Many pertinent and relevant questions cropped up in the mind of author: Why it is assumed that all children require similar education? Is not it strange that a person willing to be a sportsman, or singer or a taxi driver need to understand electro-magnetism?

To pursue career in sports, music and dance, one has to dedicate long hours starting right from childhood. Does a child dedicating life to become an Olympian need same level of science education as that of an engineer? In fact, he should be provided training in communication skills, photography, mathematics and science customized to his requirements.

In sports, time spent in puberty is very important. How can a child utilise his **energy level** and time optimally in sports and exercise without compromising with his education and career? How could a child talented in sports, music and dance cope up with both academic and sports practice sessions?

Most of the school children concentrate in development of motor skill, analytical and memory power, but lack power to think, express feeling and make presentations. How can this problem be addressed? Is the current 10+2 system of school education flexible enough to accommodate these dreams? Can we not have a separate parallel system of education for children, who wish to pursue sports, music and dance?

In India, we are still following colonial system of education. It is nothing but route learning.

NRECT has implemented various innovative techniques, but these are complicating the matter further.

As a result, we are producing millions of educated but unemployable unhappy youth.

Even IIT engineering graduates do not get attractive salary packages in core engineering sectors and diverts to other non-engineering sectors.

The author also realized that with 10+ 2 system, the children are tied down to the education system is a rigid way. In past, children had to prepare for class X exam for career selection of streams between science, arts or commerce followed by class XII exam on which admission in colleges would depend on. Recently, HRD Minister Kapil Sibbal created hype with the announcement that the school education system is being changed to ease the pressure of examination. The Xth board examination was announced to be replaced with the continuous grade system. The author was optimistic at first, when the system was replaced by **Continuous and Comprehensive Evaluation system**. But the author soon found out that for the students pursuing sports, the new system is creating more pressure compared to the earlier one. Under the new system, a student now has to take 6 exams (FA1 FA2 SA1 FA3 FA4 SA2), in place of earlier two six monthly exams. In past, a student could concentrate in practising sports and make up studies by studying just before exam. Now, he has to study throughout the year, as if studying alone is the only motive and means of life. The school in which author's son was studying, implemented two more exam called oral tests, before the main exams. In vacations, the students are not allowed time to breathe. The burdens of home works are getting extremely high and boring. No flexibility is provided in the curriculum. It would be better if students are allowed to choose their own homework in flexible way.

The author proposes a new independent flexible education system in this chapter in order to bridge the gap between the needs of the children for a holistic growth and the existing rigid curriculum based education system in India. Flexible education proposed by the author balances the academics with the hobbies, interests and likes, so that a child is able to choose what he want to pursue, excel in it right from the childhood and make it a career if possible.

1.2   Need for Flexible Education System

The need of the millennium is a flexible education system for the children, which takes our nation to a higher level of growth of all assets. Educational system of a country is always influenced in its journey of evolution by its social, cultural and historical factors. The Indian education system was modelled after British system, which gave too much impetus on the degrees and jobs. Inspite of 68 years of independence, we still carry on our back, the colonial legacy of a rigid formal system.

1.2.1   The present educational structure

The present educational system in India has an old structure and full of variations and anomalies. There are many regulatory bodies to regulate the private school systems, since there is much regional variations and heterogeneity in the system

a. **Pre-School Child Care System (0 – 3 years):** In the modern society, many times it becomes imperative for the working mothers to put their infant children in a child care home or crèche. Japan has evolved the excellent system of Hoikuen, where children of working mothers are taken care by trained childcare professionals and teachers in a holistic way. Unfortunately, in India, this is one of the most neglected sectors, with shabby places, untrained & underpaid caretakers and lack of childcare experts.

b. **Pre-primary system (3-6 years):** The present Indian education system starts at age the age of 3-4 years, with pre-primary system. This sector is the most unorganized sector with least regulations and curriculum. Most of the times, these schools are built in cramped buildings on localities and declare to be following Montessori or other teaching methodologies. But the fact is that, majority of them lack good quality and trained primary teachers. There is often no space for playground and there is no stress on flexibility exercises. Learning the alphabets, rhymes, drawing and singing becomes the primary goal.

c. **Primary and Middle School System (Class 1 to VIII):** This is supposed to be the most enjoyable part of the life. Parents want their children to perform well in studies as well as indulge in some extra-curricular activities like music, dance, art, games, etc. As the child grows, there is extreme pressure from both study and hobby. The children having special background, e.g. from business back ground or with parents from sports, music or movie back ground are luckier to get appropriate training necessary to be successful in such trade of life.

d. **Secondary School (Class IX and X):** This is the most critical stage of life that gives direction to life. The stage of puberty, the physical growth of the boys and girls are at its peak and ripe for intensive sports activities. An excellent atmosphere for sports would have created a strong body, great endurance and stamina. But unfortunately, at this stage, our education system emphasises on the academic performance. The children with latent energy for the sports and dance/music activities are supressed at this stage and they are forced to concentrate on their study.

e. **Higher Secondary School (Class XI and XII):** In our current educational system, the child has to take one of the most important decisions of the life – selection between science, arts and commerce stream. Once the decision is taken, there is no much chance of changing stream afterwards, even when the children performance is poor in the selected stream. Many children drop out and join vocational diploma courses. Students who join science, then face the next race of life: medical, engineering, or normal graduation courses. Children who join arts and commerce also have their own dilemma about career selection.

1.2.2 Misplaced Expectations and Subjects

Parents have infinite expectations with their children in performing well in the studies without bothering about the interest and aptitude of the student or about the earning capability of those streams. For example, JEE exam, for entrance to top engineering institutes like IITs, is one of the most competitive exams of India, which selects the most talented students. The author was also one of the achiever with JEE 326 rank in 1986. After Joining IIT Madras, most of the students in his batch realized that they did not want to be engineer and prefer to join MBA, IAS or IES. Very few students joined higher studies in engineering. Dr. Gupta continued to remain in civil engineering, completing his masters and doctoral studies. Author was disturbed to see the following paradoxes:

a. The country needs capable and good engineers badly.

b. The most brilliant students in our country join engineering courses, yet do not want to be engineers.

c. The starting salary for engineers from IITs is not good as MBAs from IIMs

d. The Private engineering sectors do not provide good salary to IIT Students, while banking and other sectors absorb IIT students with very attractive packages.

Hence, it is important to develop an education portal, where children get a clear picture of the future and there is proper utilization of the resources. Would it not be better if the career options, the required efforts and job-returns are known through educational portal and students spend more time more efficiently?

In life, to be successful, one needs to provide concentrated effort for 10 years. It is often seen that children from business family/artistic family do not give priority in studies but learn trade from family and become more successful. If this is true, why can't our education system provide such wide variety of education to our children?

For students pursuing sports, the subjects should also reflect the knowledge required by the individual sports. For example, a swimmer can be taught about the hydrodynamics that occurs in each of the strokes. For cricket or football, this may be related to weight, strength, momentum and swing of the ball. In biology, one may be taught about the specific muscles growth and their strength development. The child can have a maths book talking of speed of cricket/tennis balls and calculation of impacts. He will study the body strength, endurance required for sustaining his sports career. A singer or an artist would learn music possibly in a scientific way and learn about strength of vocal cord and related matters. A music loving child might learn the differences in frequency, pitch and characteristic of various musical notes. This way we would actually spend more energy in knowledge wealth creation and implementation that would help in various ways. At present, most sports and music people are not supported by present education system.

Special compensatory credits should be given by the schools, if the activities involve long hours of practice. The long hours of practice should involve some organized training of science or otherwise that can be evaluated and the results along with results of practice should be counted as part of study, with matching credits / grades equivalent to that subject's exams.

1.2.3 Requirement of long dedicated hours for Sports, Music and Dance in childhood

Sports, music and dance are forms of entertainment, which hold infinite source of employability for the students who want to pursue careers in it. Only a few of the fortunate students are able to pursue their dream of making professional career in the sports and entertainment, backed by their family resources and the professional courses. The others are unable to afford this. The star sportspersons are the product of taking to the field at an early age. The government sports programmes are unable to support many talented children. The journey to stardom starts with long hours of practice starting from very early age. A few illustrations taken out from the lives of successful sportspersons and entertainers will validate the fact that there is urgent requirement of catching the talented children young and putting them to vigorous practice sessions right from the school days.

The star gymnast, **Nadia Comaneci** of Romania won three gold medals in 1976 at the age 14. She began her gymnastics in kindergarten [Wikipedia]. At age of 10 years, she won her first national competition and soon started participating international competitions. At age of 13, she nearly swept the 1975 European Championship. In Montreal Olympics, she was a star getting- 3 gold, 1 silver and 1 bronze medal. In next Olympics at Moscow, she got 2 gold medals and 1 silver medal. She was the first person to get perfect 10 in gymnastics. This tremendous success of Nadia was a result of her very long dedicated practice hours ranging from 6 to 8 hours daily, right from her middle school.

The story of **Michael Phelps** was no different. He has won the maximum number of gold medals in swimming events in the Olympic History. He began swimming at the age of 7 years. In class VI, he was diagnosed as ADHD. At the age of 10 years, he was holding national record of his age group. At the age of 15 years, he qualified for the 2000 summer Olympics. Though he did not win a medal here, he reached the finals. In 2004 Olympics, he won 8 medals, of which 6 was gold medals with 3 Olympic record and two world records. In 2008 Olympics, he swept with all 8 gold medals with 7 world records and 1 Olympic record. Michael Phelps' great success was also due to a rigorous practise session of 3- 6 hours in pool every day, followed by 2 hours of exercise regimen.

Most of the children learning swimming under qualified trainers in India spend 4-5 hours and again 2 hours in the evening per day, for the exercise and pool practice. Even after this effort, the energy consumption would barely touch 5000 calories; approximately double that of an adult. Michel Phelps is known to have consumed 18000 calories a day, for this his diet was specially monitored and provided.

How could a child talented in sports, music and dance cope up with both academic and sports practise sessions?

Nadia Comaneci

Deepika
Padukone

Kapil Dev

Michael Phelps

Back home, star cricketer **Kapil Dev** in his active days had very high calorie and nutrition-loaded diet requirement. His energy consumption was above 12000 calories a day. The amount of food consumed directly reflects the energy spent by the child in creating a strong and flexible body with endurance that can withstand the rigour necessary sustaining the future sports world.

Deepika Padukone, one of the successful actresses and dancers of Bollywood Film industry is the daughter of national level badminton player Prakash Padukone. As a teenager, guided and coached by her father, she played badminton in national level championship. In her own words, "I would wake up at 5 in the morning, go for physical training, go to school, again go for playing badminton, and finish my homework and go to sleep". According to her 3 Ds are important – **dedication, discipline and determination**. She also received formal training in Bharatanatyam dance from childhood. Her strength, stamina and endurance helped her to be physically fit and this is visible in any of her dances including the dance in her film Ram Leela.

1.2.4   Children Pursuing Sports in Delhi

Let us look at the sports facilities in Chhatrasal Stadium in Delhi where the wrestler groups led by, Guru Satpal Singh (Padma Bhusan awardee) and Sushil Kumar (Two times Olympic medalist, Rajiv Gandhi Kel Ratna awardee)

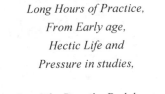

Long Hours of Practice,
From Early age,
Hectic Life and
Pressure in studies,

Just Like Deepika Padukone,
Children face a similar tough life.

are engaged in practice and coaching sessions. More than 200 children of different age groups are regularly practicing wrestling with residential facilities in this stadium. Mr. Sushil Kumar provides personal care and focussed training to the children. The children here get best of training and are very successful. The place they stay, the practice space and other facilities require serious improvement as this group represent one of the most successful group in our country.

The sporting facilities in Delhi, the national capital, are mostly located around national sports grounds developed during Common Wealth Games in 2010. These places have NIS coaches who are government employees.

A group of dedicated children is flowering, utilizing the underutilized facilities of school sports facilities. Children of the school rarely use these sports facilities in a professional way. Often private coaches and groups hire these facilities to run camps for training children willing to spend long hours, so that they can participate in state and national competitions. This is especially true for swimming.

The author had first-hand experience of witnessing the coaching programmes of dedicated school going children, when his son was passionately engaged in training to become a world class swimmer. The biggest problem was unavailability of round-year swimming pool, which hampered the training in winter. The morning and evening sessions were scheduled for the sports children. Often some children travel long distances to practice here. Children would assemble at 4.30 a.m. in the morning and do ground exercise. At about 6.00 a.m., the children would take bath and enter the pool. The swimming training would continue up to 7.00 - 7.30 a.m. Again in the evening, the children would assemble from 4.00 p.m. to 6 p.m.

The life of these children is like that of Deepika Padukone. They possibly have very little chance to enjoy their childhood with friends, torn between the school study and sports coaching. They also have to compromise with their studies. After so much hard work, there is still no future visible to the children having sports dream. The rigid educational system leaves no place and time for pursuing sports as a passion or career. Most of the children pursue sports either to get admission in colleges or get a job through sports quota. The tragic part of the story is that most children give up sports at the age of 13-15 years. This neglect of sports, music and dance in favour of studies also reflects in the lack of entertainment and health in adult life. The system glorifies children with good grades. The efforts in sports rarely count in the academics. They also have to compete with students who give least time to extracurricular activities and maximum time to studies. It basically violates the basic human rights and dignity of these children dedicating their life in sports.

The existing curriculum is not balanced. It is demanding too much from the children, who want to follow their dream of being sports champion. The curriculum would have to be designed in such a way that this would match the knowledge required for profession of sports, music and dance. The teachers in sports school should be of highest standard and be paid better, so that the children can be provided subject education in between their practice sessions of sports. For children who could not dedicate enough time to education, the education years can be extended to give them a relaxed atmosphere. Special emphasis should be provided in communication skills, science related to their field, photography, such that children not doing well can have lot of other career options. This will also make post retirement options for sports children better.

Author's son had once asked him at age of 11 years, about what would happen to him if he fails in his sports dream of becoming a champion, despite giving best of efforts under his father's guidance. This question has continuously troubled the author and made him propose a complete self-sustained system, where children can dedicate their early life in sports, music and dance without feeling scared of the future.

1.2.5 High expense of pursuing of sports, music and dance

Parents of these children pursuing sports suffer a lot. Not only do they have to support the children mentally, they have to be there and provide support in transportation. Financial burden is a bigger problem. Most sports require costly equipments. Even if we assume that these facilities are provided for, food expenses become a big problem. The food cost is very high as energy intake increases, with increase of hours of training. At present there are only few residential sports schools, supported by government, corporates, foundations and trusts, which provide all type of support to the talented sports persons. But there is no effective support system for helping financially the boys and girls, who shows potential in sports at the middle and high school level.

1.3 Proposal for Modification of Education System

The background and requirement of the changes has been explained. Children are indeed suffering with no clear picture of the future. It is very important that we do serious introspection and change the system. Some of these sections are elaborated later in separate chapters.

1.3.1 Flexibility Exercise and swimming in childhood

A child is born 9 months swimming in placenta watery fluid. Hence, all children are born swimmer. The astonishing power of children to swim has been demonstrated by various people. Hence, flexibility exercise and swimming is strongly suggested for small children. Author, observing the system in Japan and Hoikuen, realized that the first part of life, i.e. first week, first month, first year and then the first three years, shapes the brain, body and interest of the child. This is the time when bones are flexible. In either of the tree figures, the grass in the bottom represents the compulsory flexibility exercise and swimming in childhood. Music and dance also should be ingrained in the children from this stage. One should understand that healthy body is the most important asset a person can have in life. If one is tired after workout, he will also get a healthy appetite and sound sleep.

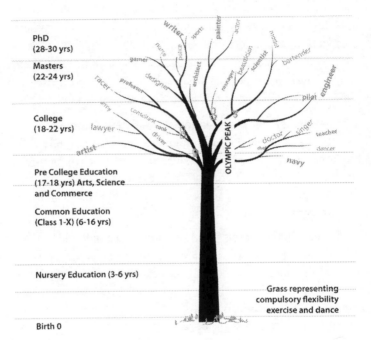

Fig 1: Existing Education System

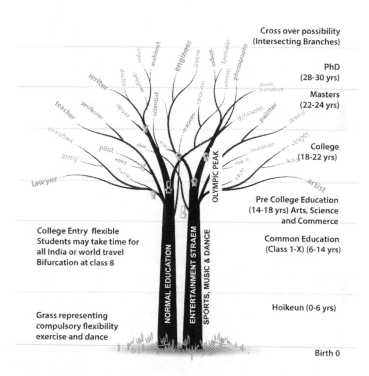

Fig 2: Proposed Education System

1.3.2 Alternate Job Opportunities

If one starts an education system for sports, music and dance, it is obvious that the percentage of children able to earn directly from sports, music and dance would be small. Even when one is successful, post retirement occupation is a serious problem. Hence, it is important to have alternate job opportunities. The branches of this tree in Fig 1 and 2 denotes alternate job opportunities of coaches, physiotherapists, photographers, journalists, amateurs, etc. The good exposure in sports, music and dance will help them be successful in these alternate professions as supporting roles. A large number of these children will also become compatible spouse for the successful cases. The contribution of these people to the success of the people who won highest laurels cannot be underestimated. Without career guarantee, no children will be ready to take risk and join this option. Most Indian films and IPL games employs foreigner dancers. Indians people trained under this entertainment stream can then imagine to be part of such opportunities like IPL dancers, dancers as in Disney Land, etc.

1.3.3 Separate Independent Curriculum

The right side of the tree in Fig 1, represent the entertainment education system, primarily for creating a self-sustained education system for people, willing to dedicate their life to sports, music and dance. Since all these are forms of entertainment, they are bundled together. It is expected that all children pursuing this career lines will have to spend more time in activities that create strength, stamina, endurance and body flexibility.

It has been highlighted that children pursuing sports, music and dance require long hours of practice in their school years. It has been elaborated that it is important for a sportsman to become a full entertainer by being able to sing and dance. Their physical agility will provide them an easy edge to become so. This will also enhance their stability in their post-retirement stage. Similarly for a singer, it is now a days becoming more important to have beautiful body with strength, stamina and endurance to be able to perform live on stage and TV programs. Hence, it is important for people pursuing music and dance to undergo sports training.

It is obvious that present education system is not good enough for these children. A separate curriculum needs to be drafted in such a way that all subjects are designed to satisfy the scientific requirements of these children. One must also keep in mind the alternate job opportunities also while drafting the curriculum. The science, maths, history subjects, taught to these children should reflect the need of activities. The teachers should provide training in between the training sessions so that the children pursuing sports, music and dance are empowered for facing the future world confidently.

Since the two systems will work parallel, there will be sharing of resources. Students would be able to cross over to the other side at all stages.

1.3.4 Bifurcation in Class VIII and Graduation Flexibility

The left side of the tree in Fig 1, depicts the conventional education system with categories of selection of specialized stream after class X. The right side of the tree in Fig. 1 or Fig. 2 depicts the proposed education system. It is proposed that the selection of science, arts and commerce be done after class VIII. The system may have other options like "Nurse" for jobs that provide large job opportunities. In villages, irrigation may also be an option.

In present system, class XI and XII are the period that determines the future and the college to which the child will get admission. This period is too short and fast. The child has no possibility to think of switching streams. Neither can he concentrate on building a strong body. In Japan and various countries, this pre-college stage of education is or a 3 years duration. This provides a better opportunity to the students.

The author believes that four years at this stage, after class VIII would be even better option. It would be good enough period for children to consider **switching over courses** if they want and make up their mind for their career stream. The main purpose is to make the children aware of various possibilities of career and life so that they choose proper stream and not crowd institutions like IITs, if they have no intention to become engineers. In this relaxed atmosphere, author also strongly encourages students to take breaks, travel and see the world before selecting college education.

Similarly, it may be noted that sportsman may not be able to provide enough time to education due to requirement of sports world. In such case, one may postpone, but not neglect the minimum education required to face the real world.

1.3.5   Sports and Education Portal

Proposal for Sports Portal has been presented in this book. This concept can be extended to music and dance too. The high expenses of parents can be subsidized by creating entertainment for public and also promoting sponsorship programmes. There might be some delay in flow of the fund in the initial stages, but once the system shows results, the inflow of funds will increase. CSR and Government support and fund will obviously flow in parallel to the public and individual support.

The proposal for Education portal will provide detailed information about all possible job opportunities available in today's life. This will help children aim for life depending on their interest and capabilities.

1.3.6   Minimum Management, Legal, Accounts and Communication Skills

The author once asked some students as to why they took engineering when they have no intention of being engineers. The students replied that the character building and mind-set that is created in the engineering course is unique. Engineering-MBA combination helps students to be more successful in life. This basically destroys the importance of having engineering colleges as building block of the nation. A minimum level of knowledge in management, law, accounts and communication skills are very important in the success of the students in their life so that they can face world with confidence.

1.4   Conclusions

The author has elaborated on various concepts of this flexible education system, many of which are discussed in other independent chapters of this book. Some of the related and relevant concepts, which are being conceived and supported by the author, are:

a.   Promote early age education (Hoikuen)

b.   Promote the importance of swimming and flexibility exercise in school curriculum.

c.   Promote the important role of entertainment including sports, music and dance in life

d.   Lowering of age for selection of line of specialization for career courses.

e.   Encourage student to take breaks, travel, and see the world before selecting college education.

f.   Availability of more career and professional courses options and knowledge through interactive education portal.

g.   Non-crowding of students to IITs and allow the students genuinely interested in engineering to join.

h.   Have total independent stream as Entertainment wing, for children willing to have a career in sports, music and dance.

i.   Easy cross over between normal and entertainment wings of education at any stage.

j.   If the concept of sports portal is successful, children who are putting extremely high efforts in sports, music and dance will be known to public and their financial needs can be taken care easily.

k.   Various supporting career options possibilities including being spouse for the non-successful children.

l.   Redefining the course curriculum of maths, science, history and other subjects depending on the need of this entertainment branch.

m.   Minimum management, legal, accounts and communication skills.

The concept of flexible education as proposed by the author, is like germination of new ideas, so that the experts, academicians and government agencies are encouraged to conduct further discussions, research and take proposed actions, on this important area of human development of our children as assets. Currently, we are lagging behind in many areas like sports, activities and research, due to our rigid education system, which gave more stress on mugging, tests and outdated subjects.

The author will sensitize the various stakeholders, so that flexible education is made part of our curriculum right from schools to colleges. The CBSE, ICSE and State Education Boards should also take initiatives to support this concept and design tailor made curriculum to implement it, keeping in mind the local context. Their curriculum should match their sports (or music, dance, art) such that they learn physics, chemistry maths or subjects of their interest.

Educational Portal

CHAPTER 2
EDUCATION PORTAL

2.1 Introduction

The middle class forms a substantial chunk of population of our country, which is primarily consisting of the working and professional classes. The primary aim of this class is to get education and then get a job. The journey of a middle class Indian from childhood to adulthood is a pathetic story of constant race for achievement. From the very childhood, a typical child faces the competition of learning alphabets, memorizing points, learning dozens of subjects and mugging up for exams. After education, he is immediately forced to take up jobs, marriage, children and then again education and career of the children.

Even in this age of internet and information explosion on career choices, youth get confused about how to select a course. So there is a need of providing web-based portal or platform, which provides qualitative information about traditional and non-traditional jobs, vocations and careers. The proposed educational portal will attempt to satisfy this need of the youth.

> **Indian educational system has become so formal and rigid, giving too much stress on academic subjects, that children are lost in Alice-in-wonderland, while making career and occupational decisions.**
>
> *Most children in this education system do not have much idea, which way their life is leading to. Most middle class students make attempts for engineering, medical MBA courses or attempting for government jobs like IAS, clerical, banking etc.*

There are so many options and choices to be made in life. Children rarely know these or consider them as healthy practical options. Once the author went to Maldives on a tour and felt

> Could we not have a career selection process, which is based on interest and aptitude of the children, so that they can enjoy their childhood and life to its fullest?

jealous of the carefree life of a scuba diving coach, working there in a resort. He was born in Europe but was then leading a fantastic life, travelling around the world, while taking coaching assignments as a scuba diver. There are lot of exciting non-traditional careers, like- Hotelier, fashion designer, photographer, journalism, chef, etc. These are various options that our children rarely think of. Even if they are aware of them, they have no information about good institutes and career opportunities existing in these fields. Sometimes, only people who are unable to get into traditional careers, get into these professions without much interest. Would it not be better world if meritorious people chose these professions based on their likings, allowing students who really want to be engineers/doctors to pursue their own dream?

The objective of this chapter is to conceptualize the development of an educational portal that provides a wide platform and window, making available information about wide range of career options, success stories, seat availability, cost of courses, talent and money required to pursue the specialized selected lines. It will cover not only courses and office jobs but also business, entrepreneur's skills and other skill development areas.

2.2 Concept

This concept note focuses on creation of a unique educational portal, as conceived by author. The proposed portal will be creating and developing an all-inclusive and integrated online educational platform. It will provide qualitative information about traditional and non-traditional vocational & career options. This portal would serve as a guide and career counsellor to the youth. The choice of the career will depend upon the aptitude, interests and capability of the students, matched by accurate information about all type of latest courses, which will be made available at the portal.

Currently, there are many educational and career portals, but most of them are providing information about the top most institutes and courses in traditional career areas only, ignoring the newly emerging courses and entrepreneurship skills. The portal has been conceived and designed keeping in mind the current problems in selecting vocations and the unmet aspirations of our people.

The Educational Portal will include the following features and services:

a. Information about alternative and non-traditional newer courses and careers in predefined categories.

b. Information about the cost, fees, time, efforts, aptitude and stamina required to complete the courses.

c. The career opportunities and scope in each of the selected courses.

d. Interactive Question and Answers links on the portal for satisfying the queries of the students and individuals, which will also involve nominal charges.

e. Publishing of success stories about different careers including entrepreneurship and business skills.

f. Reference for further website links and resource centres for educational and career related specialized information.

g. Revenue generation by advertisement by professional institutes, colleges and government supported centres.

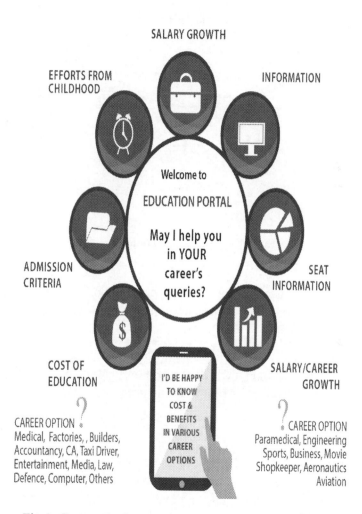

Fig 1: Career Options and Details of Education Portal

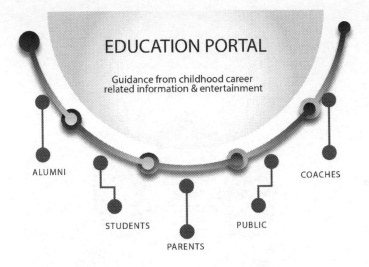

Fig. 2 Participation of various stake holder in Education Portal

h. Provision for a reader's contribution section, for sharing his experiences in different courses and careers

i. Provision for Blogs and articles by experts. It will be offbeat and interesting like -how to become politician or heroines or franchisee manager or a taxi driver.

j. There will be regular newsletter and information bulletin at the portal.

Fig 1 depicts the different career options including the non-traditional like NGO, shopkeepers, taxi drivers, entrepreneurs. The portal will cover all the detailed information about the career, including the admission criteria, fees, faculty, cost, placement, future scope and expected salary. It will help the student to take informed decisions regarding the selection of the career. Fig 2 illustrates participation of various stake holder - the Students, Parents and the general Public. The interaction will be two-way, in the form of comments, feedbacks and question answer columns. There will be also interaction from alumni of reputed institutes, professional and experts of all specialized fields.

2.3 Outcomes and Conclusions

The educational portal will make a tremendous impact on creating a choice-based and information-based career decision. It will create an atmosphere of awareness among the users. Its outcomes will be:

a. General public and students will get access to various issues relating to education and career matters on a wide platform

b. Active Participation in the portal will create more awareness among the public to take informed decisions on options of careers.

c. The interactive portal will also satisfy the queries of the students from the experts

d. The portal will be based on a sustainable fees based and subscription model, where revenues will also be generated, from both users and advertisers.

The content of the portal will be designed aiming to provide a wide window for the educational and career choices to cultivate a user-oriented platform, where the needs and aspirations of the students are shared, disseminated and given shapes at the online portal format.

Indian society is undergoing a tremendous transformation and the youth are in front of this battle of choosing a dignified and paying career. The parents have to stop forcing their children to Engineering, Medical, Government jobs, Management and lawyer careers. There are now lots of vocation, jobs, and business to choose from. The cry of the hour is to provide a net-based portal where all the offbeat and latest courses, careers and jobs options are listed and supporting career & educational guidance services are provided. It is time to stop the blind race towards few traditional careers. The proposed portal will take care of the problem in an effective manner.

Hoikeun

CHAPTER 3
HOIKUEN

3.1 Introduction

Child rearing in the early formative years of 0 - 3 and 3 - 6 age groups is one the most important developmental aspect in moulding of human

> Children are the most important asset of the country and also the most ignored and neglected.

personality. Developed countries in Asia and Europe have highly developed pre-school and day care pedagogy, which helps a child develop his potentials to optimum level, through exploring, sensory and motor activities. Traditionally in India, children in these formative years would grow in the hands of either grand-parents or of helping hands like maids or servants. In nuclear family, mother often gives up job to take care of the child. Does the mother really have the right knowledge about child growth and care? Often, the personality of the child is impacted negatively in its formative years of 0 – 6 years due to lack of knowledge about good child rearing practises.

Internationally, Child Rearing Practices (CRP), for the 0 – 6 age group, has been a fertile area of research. The relationship between overall mental and physical development of the child and CRP, however, is complex because of geographical, cultural and socio-economic differences across regions of the world. Indeed, there are common threads and themes that help in understanding the motivational aspects of CRP and their effects on children.

> Mother needs to join work for self- reliance contributing to the development of the country.

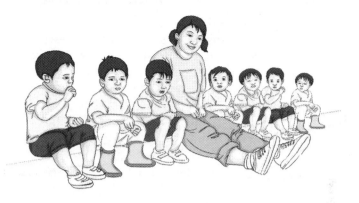

Among the Asian Countries, Japan has its own system of child rearing practices called HOIKUEN. The author Dr. Supratic Gupta had observed the Japanese practice closely during his years of stay there. Japan appreciates women to work, without compromising on the quality of companionship and the growth of the child. Child growth is one of the most important things for the country.

In Japan, firstly parents are made aware and trained about the processes and requirements of the child growth in the womb and immediately after birth. This is done by strong coordination between- medical experts, city authorities and a set of volunteers (paid or unpaid) of older experienced women, who themselves had experienced child birth and are later trained technically for this purpose. Parents have to participate in regular classes to learn the complexities of pregnancy, child birth and rearing process, during the pregnancy period of their first child is born. The medical team/ hospitals provide free health care up to 6 years of age. Regular check-ups are done in the initial years, maintaining records of body developmental index, height, dental care, etc. Women volunteers regularly visit the family to check if the mother and the family are applying the correct knowledge about child development. They also check the health, maternity and psychological needs of the mothers.

> **Hoikuen's child rearing practices**
>
> Flexibility, stability, sensory perception, motor skills, social relationship skills, exercising, toilet training and immunity development against diseases

Secondly, once the child is born and has crossed the initial period, mothers have to join back their work. Often they need to join work within 3 months to maximum 1 year. To take care of this need, a beautiful and effective child care system of Hoikuen has been developed in Japan. These well-developed practices in child care had been the cornerstone of early child rearing practices in Japan. Its effects on the moulding of overall personality are tremendous.

Hoikuen is the special child care system designed to take care of the children and allow women to work without worry. Unlike traditional concept of day care, where under-educated women participate to take care of children, or where people do part time to assist parents in western countries, this is a complete educational system for achieving holistic development of the child. This is a unique system. These are primarily geared toward the "welfare" of the child and are regulated by the Ministry of Welfare under the Child Welfare Law.

The aim of this chapter is to introduce the concept of Hoikuen, so that people in India and worldwide can do introspection for the benefit of working women and child rearing practices. Children are the most important human resources of a country that deserve more contribution in terms of investment for better future.

3.2   Concept

Hoikuen is one of the unique responses of Japan to Early childhood care in community. For more than a century, Japanese early childhood education programs have been divided into two main institutions: Hoikuen (preschool education system) and Yochien (kindergarten). Hoikuen is operated under the auspices of the Ministry of Health, Labour and Welfare that conform to the Child Welfare Law. The emphasis of Hoikuen is to take care of the infant child physically and mentally. It is meant for children whose parents cannot take care of them as they have to go to work, medical or any other reason.

On the other hand, Yochien falls under the Ministry of Education, Culture, Sports, Science and Technology for children ages between 3 to 6 years, is regulated by the Ministry of Education under the School Education Law of 1947. These schools are geared toward the holistic and integrated education of children aims to nurture and teach children the basics of compulsory education. Since Hoikuen differ from Yochien in its objective and responsibilities, the contents of Hoikuen education and entrance conditions are also different. Education and training in Hoikuen facilities are carried out by day care professionals from the point of view of welfare, while Yochien education is carried out by teachers from the point of view of education. Hoikuen provide meals and sleeping hours, and may allow children to stay for long hours depending on the need of the parents.

Only children, whose mothers are working women, are eligible for Hoikuen educational system. Infants, as young as 3 months can often be seen on the laps of Hoikuen teachers, while most children, who join it, are between age of 9 months to 1 year. On

> Hoikuen is the corner stone of Japanese character building, providing them efficient five senses, a sense of equality and sincerity.

the other hand, children of non-working mothers get admission in Yochien after age of 3. While kindergarten education is not compulsory in Japan, a majority of children between the ages of 3 and 6--attend some type of early childhood programs (Web Crews, Inc., 2009). As per the trend of last 3 decades, 70% of the Japanese children are attending Hoikuen, while rest are attending Yochien and other educational care.

As reviewed, the primary function of Hoikuen has been to accommodate children while they are apart from their parents. Presently, both public and private Hoikuen are available, with no notable difference in their costs. The Hoikuen system is very convenient for working parents, because the school hours that can be utilized are quite flexible and much longer than the Yochien system. A typical kindergarten allows children to stay up to six hours in a day, where as a Hoikuen will allow children to come early and stay late each day, depending on the parents' schedule.

In 1990, modified guidelines for child care services were enforced, and the Japanese government made a major effort to meet children's individual needs. By 1999, the Ministry of Welfare had again revised guidelines for child care services, focusing on:

a. The unification of care and education;

b. Care that respects the whole child;

c. The environment as an agent for child care;

d. Broadening child care functions; and

e. The importance of caregivers' roles

Hoikuen not only focus on the child rearing practices but also on the whole range of skills development of the child, including the flexibility, stability, sensory perception, motor skills, social relationship skills, exercising, toilet training and immunity development against diseases. This concept of Hoikuen brings homogeneity in the development of child.

In Hoikuen, children develop sensory awareness with materials such as sand, water, beans, rice, flour, dirt, pasta, oatmeal, etc. They explore and distinguish textures by sifting, pouring, comparing, measuring and experimenting with a variety of materials as well as develop mathematics concepts. One may find even a 3 month old child in the lap of the teachers even though their percentage is less. Most children join at the age of one. Children grow much better in company of other children of different ages. Various tribal groups all over the world have the concept of commune where children grow up together.

Hoikuen is the corner stone of Japanese character building, providing them efficient five senses, a sense of equality and sincerity. Hoikuen usually have an open ground, swimming pool and gardening places. The rooms usually have wooden floor.

3.3 Situation in Hoikuen
3.3.1 Normal Daily Life
In this system, the children are very young and need to learn life skills activities, like drinking, eating, sleeping, playing, interacting with each other, use toilet in a scientific way, etc. These skills and training are very important part of personality development.

3.3.2 Water
One most important part of physical development is playing in water. We all know that the foetal baby grows in water, i.e. placenta inside the womb of the mother. Hence, children usually love water. In Japan, children spend substantial time of the day in water. At home also, the child is put in water in bathtub along with the parents for about an hour. In Hoikuen, the children are put in water depending on their age. Very small children use balloon pools. Elder children get into swimming pool turn by turn with increasing age. By the age of 6 years, all children can do synchronized swimming. They also play games of searching colour balls, shaped objects under water to be able to see under water.

3.3.3 Gardening

Gardening plays an important role in the development of the five senses and leads to knowledge of growth of plants (science) and development of sense of patience and achievement. As the children plant the seeds and see them sprout and grow, it gives them a first-hand experience of the phenomena of birth and growth. As the leaves come out and flowers bloom, the children are appreciated to feel the texture and smell the fragrance, thus allowing the senses to grow. As tomatoes and other vegetables grow, the children are taught not to pluck, allowing their patience to grow. When the vegetables matures, on the final day, the children pluck the eatables and complemented by purchased materials, a feast is organized to celebrate the achievements of the gardening process. "YOSH" is the sound Japanese often say loudly holding fists tightly together as a sign of achievement.

3.3.4 Physical and mental development

Swimming plays a corner stone of physical activities in summer days. In the ground, various activities are designed in such a way that children learn balance of body. Music and songs also play an important role in the child development. Though learning through books apparently seems to have taken a backburner, children of age 6 years often have much broader education and can recite poetry as good as Indian children. This Hoikuen lays the foundation of establishing a homogenous, sincere, hardworking population that provides Japan leading edge of being a successful country.

3.3.5 Immunity

In winter and summer, children often are found to playing barefoot. In very cold winter with 0 – 5 degree temperature, teacher were once asked by author, whether the children would not fall sick in such harsh conditions. The teacher answered that that exactly this was the intention, so that children should fall sick under monitored harsh conditions, so that they could develop their immune system to lead a happy and healthy adult life.

3.4   Growth of Children in Hands of Trained Teachers

Hoikuen could be better understood if it is compared in context of the ongoing research on Child Rearing Practices (CRP) worldwide in different cultures. Research on CRP has helped formulate questions on parenting styles, parents' attitude and learning on child rearing, etc. One international comparative study found that there are cultural differences in maternal parenting styles as well as toddlers' developmental outcomes depending upon factors like the amount of body contact, body stimulation, face-to-face interaction and mutual eye contact (Keller et al., 2004). Another such comparative study between Cameroon, India and Germany focusing on early developmental phase of infancy found a number of differences and commonalities in child rearing practices. In a particular community of Cameroon, the aim of child rearing is to inculcate the moral values of obedience, respect of authority and conformity to the group. Children's socialization is considered to be an instrument of the society; accepting social responsibility, commitment and involvement for the communal good such as harmony and group stability and is embedded in a highly expressive interactional exchange. Mothers have primary responsibility for child care. (Keller et. al 2004a). For the Indian community, the Hindu way of life implies substantial inter-generational distance between parents and children. The ideology prescribes absolute moral authority of parents over their children, with complete conformity and obedience to the parents as the foremost duty of children. Respect to the elder members of the family, compliance and dutifulness are the explicit socializing instructions. There is a clear hesitation on part of the mother to express too much of love and affection towards the child in the presence of others. In contrast, the infants in the German situation are expected to spend time alone or entertain themselves with toys from early age, in order to give the mother some free time for herself. There are hardly any other caregivers available because relatives usually do not live in the neighbourhood and other babysitters have to be paid. Independence from the parent is thus the major socialization goal of infancy (Keller 2007). The concepts of God and religion are also developed in the children mostly on the basis of maternal God concepts (Roos et al. 2004).

3.5   Implementation Challenges in Indian Context

If we compare the situation in India with that in Japan, the differences are astonishing. Children, coming out of Hoikuen system, have great flexibility and participate in wide range of sports. Japan, like India, also emphasizes education. Since Japan

Adults should indulge in sports, mountain climbing, going to sea-beach, swimming pool regularly.

Only then children would also participate in exercise in a natural way.

considers children almost like an asset, great importance is given to holistic education. The infrastructures of the schools are uniform throughout the country. The society is also not segregated based on economic lines. Not only children, even adults indulge in sports, climbing mountains, going to sea beaches, swimming pools are a regular matter. As a result, more growing children participate in exercises to a large extent. Since most of the people participate, this creates a parallel economy providing jobs to large number of people.

If one watches web, one can find that the children in other countries are participating in sports, dance and other physical activities showing dynamic behaviour of the people there in the comparison to our country. These matters require drastic changes in our society to have a healthy country. And this should start from childhood.

Like Japan, we also need to encourage women to work. Hoikuen is the best system that can ensure that the child gets the best of care as he will be in the hands of trained mothers getting good salary, while the parents would be able to work without any worries about their children wellbeing and upbringing. We have to research more to know, children growth under existing child care system between 0-6 age group in India stand in comparison to many other developed countries including Japan. While the life of children in these developed countries is spent more in the overall development of the health of the body, in India children grow more spending time with books. The quality of education also depends on economic background of the child. This is reflected in the overall attitude of the people in this country.

The author, in his twelve years of experience staying in Japan, always used to wonder about the success of Japan and about their sincerity and integrity. After his son was born, he realized Hoikuen to be the corner stone of Japanese character building, providing them efficient five senses, a sense of equality and sincerity. Japanese schools have a large open ground, and a large wooden floor facility to take care of indoor and outdoor games. The wooden floor also serves as an excellent place for flexibility development exercises. In Japan, unlike in Hoikuen, swimming pools are not so common in the school. Japanese people inherently love water, society has swimming pools almost everywhere. The proximity to sea also gives them extra entertainment.

The author realized that while most schools in India have started realizing the importance of having swimming pool, the importance of small children rolling over the mat and jumping over the horse, parallel bar, hanging rings can never be underplayed. Most residential boarding schools generally have better sports facilities compared to other schools.

The Indian society is quite different from the Japanese society. It will be quite challenging to implement the Hoikuen child rearing model too in India. But we can at least take out some measures and make people and government policy makers aware about its importance in developing the overall personality, strength and flexibility among the children in the early formative years. It will help us in producing a new generation of mentally and physically healthy children, who could turn out at world class sportsmen and excellent social persons. The author at initial level would suggest introducing it step-by step.

There is need of conducting and promoting more research studies in child rearing and child development in 03-06 year, to understand the relevance of Hoikuen to Indian context.

There will be an Advocacy Campaign to sensitize the people and policy makers, the importance of adapting Hoikuen to Indian Context.

A network will be built with the Government Women and Child development departments, UNICEF and leading Child Development institutes and agencies, to develop a Training Module for training the primary teachers, child care workers

and social work professional in the Hoikuen concept and its implementation.

There will be a separate training module for the mothers, grandmothers, volunteers, for the Hoikuen based child rearing practices. It will be supported by the government as well as civic society organisations and other non-governmental organisations. It will act a catalyst to its propagation. It will be also propagated with the help of Schools, NGO's and Social workers.

After developing the pilot projects with the support from government and other organisations/ institutes, we can ask the Central Government, to integrate it with Integrated Child Development Schemes (ICDS), running all over India, through Aaganwadi Centers(5). The Aanganwari Sewikas and Sahayika, could be trained in its modules. Similarly, we could advocate it to be made part of Teachers Training curriculum in India.

The Hoikuen model of Child rearing could be introduced in all the Government and private run Crèches, child care institutions and orphanage. Children in Pre-schools, Crèches and Child care should indulge more in outdoor sports, swimming, gymnastics, PT exercises climbing mountains, going to sea beaches, in early ages.

Parents need to be taught the processes and requirements of the child growth in the womb and immediately after birth. This is done by strong coordination between medical experts, city authorities and a set of volunteers (paid or unpaid) of older experienced women who themselves have experienced child birth and are later trained technically for this purpose. Parents have to participate in regular classes to learn the process when their first child is born. Teachers and Social workers could learn the concept and adapt it in their work. A professional class of experts could lead this movement, with their constructive contributions.

References

1. Heidi Keller, Relindis Yovsi, Joern Borke, Joscha Ka¨rtner, Henning Jensen, and Zaira Papaligoura (2004), Developmental Consequences of Early Parenting Experiences: Self Recognition and Self-Regulation in Three Cultural Communities; Child Development, November/ December 2004, Volume 75, Number 6, Pages 1745 – 1760

2. Simone A. de Roos (2004a), Young Children's God Concepts:Influences of Attachment and Socialization in a Family and School Context, Researcher in Educational Sciences, Department of Philosophy and History of Education, Free University Amsterdam

3. Heidi Kellermonika Abelsbettina Lammrelindis D. Yovsisusanne Voelkeraruna Lakhani, (2005) Ecocultural Effects on Early InfantCare: A Study in Cameroon, India, and Germany, ETHOS, Vol. 33, No. 4, pp. 512–541, ISSN 0091-2131, electronic ISSN 1548-1352

4. Keller, H. (2007). Cultures of infancy. Mahwah, NJ: Erlbaum

5. http://wcd.nic.in/icds/icdsteam.aspx.

Swimming & Exercise
for flexibility

CHAPTER 4
SWIMMING AND EXERCISES FOR FLEXIBILITY

4.1   Introduction

A child born today is the future asset of the country. Our country should recognize it and dedicate all its energy to improve the health, growth and future of the child. The process of holistic growth and development starts right from

Life is movement, stay alive. Flexibility exercises that develop your full range of movement will help you on the slopes as well as in daily life.

-Adrian Crook

infancy period to early childhood. Successful participation and excellence in sports, to reach a world class performance, requires a good foundation of developed mind and body, starting from the time a baby is born. Thus, 0-6 years, the formative years, becomes the foundation stone of a healthy mind in a healthy body. India urgently needs to understand the importance of flexibility exercises and water games in the formative years of the children to create a healthy country. We have cross-cultural examples of introducing these in the developed countries of Asia, Europe and America. When an infant passes through the journey of life, from womb to birth, it throws its legs and hands, while crying aloud. Thus, starts the beginning of flexibility exercises. In India, our traditions has preserved the art of oil massaging, kept alive by the

India urgently needs to understand the importance of flexibility exercises and water games in the formative years of growth of the children to create a healthy country.

The formative period – 0 to 6 years is the foundation stone for the future.

grandmothers and elders, which are a complete set of flexibility exercises of limbs and muscles groups of the baby. But the new nuclear family mothers are not aware about its nuances. Here, most children would grow in the hands of either grand-parents or helping hands like maids or servants. In nuclear family, mother often gives up job to take care of the child.

Does the mother really have adequate knowledge about child growth and care? Is she aware of the role of flexibility exercises and aquatics exercises, which are so prevalent in Japan and other developed countries? Often, the personality of the child is reinforced in its formative years of 0 – 3 years. The physical exercises determine the sports culture of that country. India is performing poorly in international sports due to neglect of exercises and organised outdoor games in the early childhood period. The early formative years of 0-3 and 3-6 age groups is one the most important developmental aspects in moulding of human personality and attitudes. Developed countries in Asia and Europe have highly developed Pre-school and day care pedagogy, which helps a child develop fully his potentials, through activities including exploring, sensory and motor perceptions.

The author Dr. Supratic Gupta had observed the Japanese practices of baby exercises closely during his years of stay here. Japan appreciates women to work, without compromising on the quality

> To become world class sportsperson, one requires strong foundation of mind and body developed right from birth.

of companionship and the growth of the child. Child growth is one of the most important things for the country. Parents need to be taught the processes and requirements of the child growth in the womb and immediately after birth. He was much impressed by important role being played by flexibility exercises, gymnastics and water sports in the early formative years of the infant children.

He also observed the Japanese child care system of Hoikuen, which promotes healthy mental and physical growth among children, including the flexibility, stability, sensory perception, motor skills, social relationship skills, exercising, toilet training and immunity development against diseases, providing them development of all five senses, a sense of equality and sincerity. Japanese schools have a **large open ground** and a **large wooden floor facility** to take care of indoor and outdoor games. The wooden floor also serves as an excellent place for flexibility development exercises.

> *Movement is the medicine for creating change in person's physical, emotional and mental state.*
>
> *~~~Carol Welch*
>
> *It is exercise alone that supports the spirits and keeps the mind in vigour.*
>
> *~~~ Cicero*

In this concept paper, the author will highlight the importance of swimming, flexibility and other floor exercises in the development and growth of the children in early childhood as prevalent in Japan and other developed countries. We will also advocate its awareness and introduction in India, after adapting it to Indian situations and conducting research on its usefulness. There will be an attempt to make it popular among all the stakeholders, including the mothers, Play school teachers, nurses, government and other social organizations.

> *India lacks the awareness about the importance of aquatic exercise of children and need proper infrastructure, large wooden floor indoor space, playground and swimming pool.*

4.2   Swimming in Early Childhood

For a baby, the movement and exercises starts at mother's womb. It approximates to swimming in the placenta fluid in the womb. In Japan, the author observed the great wonder of teaching baby swimming, at the age of even 3 months. It seems so natural for the baby to adapt to swimming. Mothers make sure that the children spend substantial time of the day in water. At home, the child is put in water in bathtub along with the parents for about an hour. In Hoikuen, the children are put in water depending on their age. Very small children use balloon pools. Elder children get into swimming pool turn by turn with increasing age. By the age 6, all children can do synchronized swimming. They also play games of searching colour balls, shaped and colour objects under water to be able to see. Similarly in USA, Sweden, Germany, France and Italy, Children are put in water games in tubs and pools, even before they learn to walk, Aquatic games and equipment's are in great demand. Swimming is a complete exercise for the children. It also serves as the foundation of other sports.

In Indian context, there is no much awareness about the importance of aquatic exercises of children. One reason may be the dearth of swimming pools. But even then we can put the babies in bath tubs, inflated pools etc. for some period. It is a great exercise and will build up the flexibility, stamina and balance strength. We will try to make the people more aware about the benefits of water related exposures of children.

4.3   Exercise for Flexibility in Early Childhood

In Japan, the author was much impressed by the stress given on the different flexibility and floor exercises for the children from 0-6 years the formative age. Paramount importance is being given on gymnastics, the mother of all other sports and foundation fountain of a healthy and flexible body, lifelong.

Similarly in other developed countries, much importance is being given on yoga, floor exercises, balance bar, and martial arts. If one watches web, one can find out the children in other countries are participating in sports, dance and other physical activities showing dynamic behaviour of the people there in the comparison to our country.

The situation in most of the pre-schools and homes/ residential areas is not satisfactory in our country. There is lack of awareness about these activities. Only some indoor games and outdoor activities are undertaken. There is lack of trained physical teachers and infrastructures. In comparison, Japanese schools have a large open ground, and a large wooden floor facility to take care of indoor and outdoor games. The wooden floor also serves as an excellent place for flexibility development exercises. Swimming pools are rare in our schools. However, since Japanese people inherently love water, society has swimming pools almost everywhere. The proximity to sea gives them extra entertainment.

4.4   Proposed Interventions for Implementation

There is great need of highlighting the importance of swimming, flexibility and other floor exercises in the development and growth of the children in early childhood. We can learn a lot from the practices as prevalent in Japan and other developed countries. There will be an *Advocacy Campaign* to sensitize the people and policy makers, the importance of these activities. We will also advocate its awareness and introduction in India, after adapting it to Indian situations and conducting research on its usefulness. There will be an attempt to make it popular among all the stakeholders, including the mothers, Play school teachers, nurses, government and other social organizations.

We also propose to make some of these flexibility exercises compulsory for all children below a certain age. It is preferable to have wooden floor and indoor sports facility. There is need of conducting and promoting more research studies in flexibility exercises and water-based sports for early childhood age. There can be a separate training module for the mothers, grandmothers, volunteers. It will be propagated with the help of Schools, NGO's and Social workers. Once more people participate in flexibility exercises, selection based on talent and interest would be easy. Children in Pre-schools, Crèches and Child care should indulge more in outdoor sports, swimming, gymnastics, PT exercises climbing mountains, going to sea beaches, in early ages.

DISCLAIMER: AUTHORS DO NOT TAKE ANY RESPONSIBILITY FOR THE EXERCISES SUGGESTED IN THIS CHAPTER. IF ONE TRIES IT WITHOUT PROPER RESEARCH AND EXPERT GUIDANCE, HE WILL BE RESPONSIBLE FOR THE CONSEQUENCES HIMSELF

Multimedia Based Sports Portal

CHAPTER 5
MULTIMEDIA BASED SPORTS PORTAL

5.1   Introduction

The dismal status of Indian sports in domestic as well as international arena is a matter of great concern. Lot of post-mortems had been done and plenty of drastic suggestions have

> The dismal status of Indian sports in domestic and international arena is a matter of great concern.

been given by sports professionals and experts and diagnosis provided underlying the various causes responsible for this sorry state of affairs. Some sociologists and experts blame lack of sports culture in India, due to various reasons. The sports culture is also affected by different social, economic and cultural factors.

The author had first-hand observation of the current state of sports coaching, facilities and infrastructure, when he was engaged in his passion to build the Olympian career of his son in swimming. The resultant failure due to faulty coaching and educational system, led to some deep introspection by the author and suggestion of new path breaking concept, to improve the sports coaching scenario.

In the field of professional sports, there is a big gap between available expertise and available talents. While most of talents generally come from rural areas, the coaches and experts are concentrated in the cities. The whole sports coaching and training is based upon expertise of handful of coaches, who are limited in numbers. Moreover, there is no dissemination of the systematic record keeping of the training and videography of the sports activities. There is also lack of sharing of knowledge and expertise, with remote sports centres.

It is ironical that poor from the villages and small towns are taking up sports as a career option while the middle class children are not attracted towards it. This is primarily driven by the economic gain and its worthiness as perceived by these groups. In contrast, the coaches want to be in the city to provide good education to their children and enjoy other facilities in the city. The concepts proposed will create a common platform to bridge the gap between all stakeholders, including the sportspersons, coaches, sports bodies and the government and non-government agencies.

Even if we take up individual facilities in sports, rarely we find state-of-art technologies, professional medical and psychological support available. More importantly, there are few video recordings of the sport activities, which can track the progress of the sportsmen progress and which can be shared with other rural sports centres. There is no effective network, platform and medium for shared learning and getting feedbacks from experts and coaches.

In order to create a bridge between the needy people and the qualified coaches and technical experts, the author proposes to demonstrate and evolve a multi-media based training system, where advanced video recording system, meant for sports background with high speed photography can be mass produced and implemented throughout the country. This initiative will create a viral effects on all those centres, by increasing their access and outreach to quality training. Without scientific support, psychological backup or financial help, the overall success in the international level are limited.

5.2 Concepts

In this concept, a web platform is created, where sports participants, parents, outside appreciators, sponsors and coaches, are connected with others, in a financially sustainable way. Multimedia systems, including video recording and reviewing system becomes the key to this concept. It is assumed that Indian Government and the society would understand the importance of such recording system in sports and implement it is all sports bodies. This will serve the following purpose:

a. Continuous monitoring of activities of sports participants and create accountability.

b. Self-review of body movement, realization of errors and comparison with professionals.

c. Evaluation by national and international experts to form the distance guidance system.

d. Source of entertainment for paid readers and a source of information for new sportsperson.

e. This will serve as a platform, where sportspersons will be getting proper evaluation and individuals, companies and government can decide to sponsor them.

f. Beneficiary to pay either by themselves or by sponsorship.

g. Sponsors can evaluate whom they are sponsoring and evaluate their performance

h. Information related to physical development with age, correct food habits, exercise etc.

The concept of multi-media based coaching system can be integrated with the Educational network providing the following:

i. Information about educational seats in different colleges in India and abroad

ii. Information of career options after graduation

iii. Stories of successful people.

Finally it will also have information related to good branch out options for not-so-successful sportspersons. These sportsperson are expected to be better support staff, friends and spouses for the sportspersons. Lives of sportsperson require high dedication, sacrifice and lead a lonely life. A not-so successful person will be able to understand his feeling better.

Figure presents the schematic diagram of this model. At the central core, we have the sports participants. Recording would be done to document practice sessions, food habits and growth of each sports person. These videos would be uploaded on the portal site. These uploaded videos would be accessible to selected national and international coaches, medical doctors and psychologists for advice. These professional advices would be paid. The videos will also be available to all participants on a paid basis. The videos would also be viewed by well-wishers, government and private bodies. They would serve as the main financial support. They can either support in general or even support a particular sportsman for his performance. This way, good sports man would have enough credits that would help him pay for his downloads and other expenses.

This would form part of tree structure of the Chapter 1 Flexible Education. In the bottom of the tree, we have all the children practicing swimming, flexibility exercises, dance and music. As the children grow, capability and interest would be understood. As has been explained, sports, music and dance students would be put in special curriculum and the advantages of flexible education system. The children in sports would be expected to give maximum time in sports and only a few would reach the top. The dropout would be expected to still be there in the world of sports as supporting trades of physical trainer, sports journalism, coach, etc. and last and not the least as a understanding spouse.

5.3 Implementation Steps

To implement this concept is a herculean task. It requires deep understanding, cooperation, trust of system to protect intellectual and financial rights and responsibility. Hence, it is proposed to conduct a pilot project with following steps:

MULTIMEDIA BASED SPORTS PORTAL

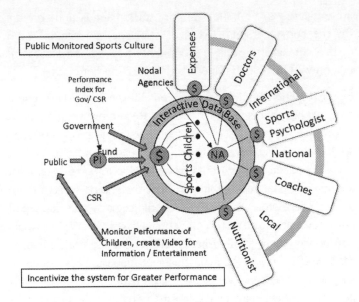

a. Identify a Central Sports Node which understand this concept, have experience in video technology, and take a lead role.

b. Central Sports Node will identify and organize a Support Body of national and international coaches, dieticians, doctors, psychologists and other experts.

c. Central Sports Body will identify and organize 4-5 enthusiastic Sports nodes representing at least two sports in rural and urban settings.

d. Provide High Speed Video recording system and other essentials technologies to each sports node.

e. Create a Portal, where data and video of practice, performance, growth, food habit and other details are uploaded in digital and video format.

f. Support Body provides distance guidance and in return gets paid.

g. Public can watch development of each child on the portal and support financially or by positive vote creating a rating. CSR and Govt. can provide support based on this public rating.

h. Sports Children can use this money any way they like, including payment to coaches and guidance. Can partially take home this money assigned to them.

The important steps for the initial trials are:

i.   Identify a Central Sports Node who understand this concept, have experiences in video technology, and take a lead role.

ii. Identify a company or that makes and runs the computer Portal.

iii. Identify funding organization. Later, the portal becomes self-sufficient.

iv. Identify Public evaluators and provide fund from project fund for trail of this model. In parallel, the system will be open to public. Success will be gauged by true public support.

A management team will be created. Central Sports Body, Portal Developer and Sponsor to create a Central Management Team of professionals, which include Dr. Supratic Gupta, Faculty IIT Delhi as an advisor and his representative from Company/NGO for management. The Central Management team will organize, control and implement the projects. The website development would also be a big step. The uploaded videos would be visible to:

a. Participants on paid basis

b. Public, private and government bodies to generate funds

c. Sports doctors, psychologist and coaches for guidance, and it is expected that they will get payments.

Good participants would automatically get funded and get credit, based on which all their life expenses would be taken care. In fact, it would be expected that they would save money.

It can also be later linked to creation of stories, multi-media documents and later a sports education portal to facilitate the information availability about dedication necessary, career possibilities, existing facilities and tournaments dates. Since most effective action is only possible by government bodies, author plans to sensitize the government of these issues and take steps of creating prototype multi-media based system and a sports education portal to facilitate the information availability about dedication necessary, career possibilities, existing facilities and tournaments dates.

5.4 Conclusion

This Chapter has presented the concept of development of a Multimedia based sports coaching system. This model is expected to link the sports persons in all places with national and international coaches with support from doctors and psychologists. This will automatically generate funds from public, private companies and government bodies. To start with, a prototype implementation is proposed under the guidance of the author.

Music & Dance

CHAPTER 6
MUSIC AND DANCE

6.1   Introduction

Music, song and dance are synonymous with the advancement of refined taste of human civilisation and possibly constitute the oldest forms of entertainment known to humankind. Animals and birds also enjoy rhythmic movements

> *Mass participation in music, song and dance would satisfy a greater need of social interaction. This will bridge the mental and community gaps that exist in most sections of people in India.*

and dance, more particularly during their courtship rituals. Scientist J. C. Bose showed that even plants enjoy music. The authors feel that mass participation in these forms of entertainment in group-mode, would provide appropriate venue for social interaction, mental peace and even physical exercise (dance), to people of all ages. This will create an atmosphere, which will also help in dilution of mental stress, as people will get a chance to interact and discuss their problems with others. Many researches and studies have suggested that group-form of entertainment satisfy the socialization needs of people. In fact, in many countries, this is accepted and practiced way of life. But in India, these types of activities, exist mostly in religious rituals, as group activities and can be categorised as follows:

a)   Prayers and devotional songs in most religions

b)   Folk/tribal music

c)   Devadasi and other forms

d)   Professional groups

We need to understand a detailed history and traditions of how people learned these entertainment forms; what percentage of people participates and how recent technology could play an important role. In Indian Music and Dance forms, traditional Gharanas existed and carried forward the legacy of music in traditional ways. But this Guru Parampara and Gharana system is getting weakened. At present, learning of music and dance is sometime reduced to hiring of private tutors at home and attending hobby classes at schools and institutes. Only a few lucky ones reach the top class performance in these activities. Most people merely enjoy hearing or watching songs/music/dance. As a result, these forms of entertainment are losing their importance to satisfy greater socialization needs.

6.2   Objectives

The objectives of this Chapter are to promote and initiate discussion on these issues:

a.   To understand and appreciate the role that music, song and dance played in past and present in other countries as compared to India.

b.   Understand how religious organizations and rituals utilize these entertainment forms for the socialization needs.

c.   Understand how these entertainments are utilized to satisfy the socialization needs of people in a financially sustainable manner in other countries.

d.   Initiate discussion among academic people, media, musicians, dancers and other performers, on whether these forms of entertainment can be used to create forums to satisfy the socialization needs.

e.   To explore the possibility of empowering children and all sections of the society to express their inner feelings through writing songs and creating music by following simple modules. If we cannot empower people to write songs, how do we expect a selected few to represent their true voice?

However, the objective of this write up is to explain to people our concepts, so that they can decide to participate more to make this activity a success.

6.3 Background and Review

The dance and music reflects the higher refinement of human civilisation. Even in the stone-age, drawings of group dances performed by men and women are found in the walls of the caves. The community singing and group dances evolved all over the world in different forms. Most culture and countries have their own cultural forms of dances and music. In other countries, the proportion of people who learn song/music/dance is much larger than in India. This section presents different scenario that can form the food for thought for Indian people.

6.3.1 Dance and Music in Japan

Japan, like India has a long tradition of different forms of classical as well as modern dances. Kabuki is a classical dance-drama. Bon Odori is a dance to welcome the spirt of the dead, performed in mid-August. Large number of people usually dances around a wooden platform called Yogura. In end, colourful lanterns are floated on water bodies for the spirit to return. This is a very colourful festival. Japanese people usually have very enjoyable life, full of dance, music and festivals.

Other than such big festivals, Japanese people organize local parties in almost every possible occasion with large dance parties with elaborate food arrangements: New Year, Christmas, summer festivals, winter festivals, etc. These parties are mostly secular in nature. Christmas is celebrated with no fixed dates. Santa Claus arrives carrying gifts to the children. Since the prayer is missing, the parties are more fun.

Another important system that make the Japanese life enjoyable is the system of **Karaoke**, which give the people a chance to sing songs in a closed environment, with good sound system, along with accompanying music. Now days, we enjoy the stereophonic high quality music inside the car.

6.3.2 Music in Dr. Gupta's life in RKM Vidyapith Deoghar and home

The authors had spent their childhood in a residential school, Ramkrishna Mission Vidyapith, situated in Deograh, Jharkhand. It had excellent sports and other activities facilities. There were wide choices available to students; one could do gardening or learn music or just join a Vedic prayer group. Unlike many other students, Dr. Gupta was never attracted to learn song or music in formal way, and failed to understand the sense of beats.

Despite this, he enjoyed music in two particular situations. There were prayers compulsory for all students every morning and evening. He enjoyed these prayers, despite the fact that he was an agnostic and never prayed to God. He was also a sincere participant of Vedic Chant groups, as it involved chanting in groups. The small curious child found the sound of OM and other Vedic chants very soothing and magical.

During vacations, Dr. Gupta would sing along with songs played on record players, alone. He never expected any appreciation from any one. It was much later in his life, that he encountered the meaning of rags (musical notes), beats of drums, Salsa and Bachata dances and understood the beauty of dance and music in life. He does not feel shy to sing songs and entertain other, even though he does not have a very melodious voice. In parties, he usually sparks other talented people to sing as he acts as an ice breaker.

6.3.3 Dance and Music in Church

Church is a place most Christian gather, meet people and share your feelings. In modern society, it is difficult to get an occasion to meet each other. Many churches designate separate times for different social and age groups to assemble. In the name of God, there is mass music and song, for which regular session are organized. The varieties of music that is developed in all languages are amazing.

6.3.4 Traditions of Dance and Music in India

India has the highest tradition of dances, including the Bharatanatyam, Kathakali, Kathak, Kuchipudi and Oddisi. Mostly girls learn these dance forms for individual excellence and artistic expression. On the other hand, India has rich tradition of folk and tribal dances. Unlike classical dances, here

larger participation of masses is noticed. Garba, Gagari (dance), Ghodakhund & Dandiya in Gujarat, Kalbelia, Ghoomar, Rasiya in Rajasthan, Neyopa, Bacha Nagma in Jammu and Kashmir, Bhangra & Giddha in Punjab, Chholiya dance in Uttarakhand, Bihu dance in Assam, Sambalpuri Dance in Western Odisha, Manipuri and Mizoram dances, etc. are present in their glorious forms. Despite such rich traditions, there is a severe scarcity of group music and dance. Most of the times, we learn music in small groups. As a result, the quality in improvement is low and rate of dropout is high. Punjab is the only state where almost each and every one can dance Bhangra. It may look simple and easy, but it requires great physical fitness.

6.3.5 Dance and Music Elements in Indian Festivals

Dance and Music is inherent part of any social culture, but the intensity and popular participation of general masses vary from place to place. India has also rich traditions of festivals and local celebrations, which utilize dance and music as instruments of social cohesion, cultural identity and mass entertainment. But the degree of participation of people is different from many other cultures.

India is a land of great cultural diversity and each state and region has its own unique religious festivals and functions. In Bengal, the festival of Durga Puja is great time of celebration, where dance, singing and other events are held in Pandals. Cultural festivals are also carried out where both professional and local groups perform. Elders and Children practice for long time to provide performance. Arati completion is just a type of electrifying dance competitions Other festivals like Sarwaswati Puja, Kali Puja, Lakshmi Puja are also celebrated just as point of social gatherings. Similarly the Dandiya dance in Gujarat and Maharashtra during Navaratri and Holi festivals in north India has great dance and music elements. During Dandiya, the recent trends show some elements of mass music and dance, with active participation of the general masses. Similary Lohri and Baishakhi of Punjab, Fagua of East UP / Bihar and Bihu of Assam have mass music and dance involvement in limited context. The tribal traditions of Music and Dance in different states have also reasonably good participation of people. All these festivals provide feeling of cultural identity and assertion.

The popular festivals usually provide best opportunity to socialize and enjoy life. Although all the above dance and music participation involves general masses in different ways, most of these activities do not qualify as mass music and dance. It lacks the energy of the mass activities and also the euphoria that the mass music and dance provides. The only exception is the day of immersion ceremony of the idols in Durga Puja, Ganesh Chathurthi and some tribal dances, where people dance and sing in all wilderness and abandonment, providing the happiest atmosphere.

6.3.6   Bhakti Traditions and ISKON

The roots of mass dance and music in Indian religious traditions go back to the times of Atharva Veda (the hymns), Nataraja (The Dancing God) and Dancing girl statue of Harappan civilisation. Even during the Mauryan period in 600 BC, many ancient republics had Spring festival called" Madanotsava", where men and women danced in gay abandon, in honour of "Kamdeva", the God of Love.

Though there were many traditions of devotional mass dance and music in different sects, the worship of Vasudeva and later the Avataars of God Vishnu- Rama and Krishna, gave rise to Vaishnavism. It involves participation of people in music, sankirtana and dance. Vaishnavism is also infused with elements of 'bhakti, an intense form of devotion to a personal God, to whom we surrender completely. The Bhakti process is laid down by Lord Sri Krishna in Bhagavad Gita and later revived by many social and religious reformers in medieval period.

Vaishnava music was extremely influential in the evolution of Indian musical tradition. In the 14th century, Amir Khusro, who spent some time in the court at Bengal, was exposed to the Vaishnava tradition and carried it to the Delhi Sultanate stronghold in Northern India. The devotional and spiritual songs of Mira, Tulsidas, Surdas and many other Sufi saints further enriched it and connected it with the masses. With the rise of Vrindavana, 14th century onwards, there was an admixture of the strains of devotional music from different regions of India. Followers of Vallabhacharya of Andhra and Nimbarkacharya of Maharashtra rubbed shoulders with Vaishnava composers from Bengal and Bihar, who owed their inspiration to Shri Chaitanya Mahaprabhu. Shri Chaitanya built up a devotional movement in eastern India, which witnessed mass sankirtana and exuberant dance by followers. This musical tradition continues to be popular in Bengal with the Bauls. The traditions of songs and music developed in Bauls groups are modern, witty, rhetorical and with strong social message. However, sadly, the Bengalis society merely sit and enjoy these songs being played on stage.

The other kirtan-based groups from the medieval ages include Qawwalis groups supported by Sufi sects, where both Hindus and Muslims participated fully. Kirtana, a form of devotional call-and-response chanting, first popularized by Sri Chaitanya Mahaprabhu, was given a fresh lease of life by ISKCON. Srila Prabhupada, the founder of ISKCON, had made mass music and dance popular all over the world. The ISKCON devotees follow a disciple line of Gaudiya Bhagavata Vaishnavas[1, 2]. Often kirtan begins slowly and melodiosly with simple rhythmic beats, gradually building up to a greater complexity and then peaking with exuberant singing and dancing. These songs are devotional songs depicting the love between Radha and Krishna. People sing Bhajans in the loudest of voices and often dance in ecstasy and abandon without rules and restrictions. Dancing is also done gracefully in front of the Lord.

Many ISKCON devotees have shared dynamic musical expressions and become accomplished singer and musicians. Srila Prabhupada's disciple, Havi das aka Ilan Chester received the Latin Grammys for "best folk or traditional album of the year" for his collection "Tesoros de la música Venezolana"(Treasures of Venezuelan Music). ISKCON temples regularly host stage performances and provide dance lessons. Bhakti Kalalayam (Devotional Arts Refuge) Academy in Alachua Florida is one such place known for its contributions.

Though the dance and music is clubbed with devotion to God, its efforts in this direction is really appreciable. Even though we find ISKCON temples at all places, they are not gaining the popularity they deserve, as Indian people are looking forward to more secular atmosphere. Vaishnavism originated in Bengal/Orissa region. Yet it did not become popular in this region due to its vegetarian philosophy. Bengalis primarily believe in balanced non-vegetarian food, where they eat large quantity and varieties of vegetable, pulses, and small quantity of fish/meat or egg.

These tradition of using mass music and dance is existent in Indian traditions, but not popularised due to their limited restricted appeal and rigid regulations. We have to popularise the ISKCON model, in its secular adopted forms, so that more and more people join it. Its exercise and mental relaxation factors should not be ignored in modern time.

6.3.7 The Art of Living

The most successful story of implementing music and dance, is the great experimental work being done by The Art of Living

> ISKCON and Art of Living have implemented mass music and dance nicely.

foundation, founded by eminent spiritual Guru Sri Sri Ravi Shankar. Initiated in 1981, the Art of Living is an educational, spiritual and humanitarian movement, engaged in stress-management and service initiative. It is successful in satisfying in fulfilling the greater need of social interaction and lessening of stress and complexities of life [3].

The Art of Living is a multi-faceted organisation with one of the largest volunteer bases in the world, with network in 137 countries. This movement has spread peace across communities through diverse humanitarian projects, including conflict resolution, disaster relief, sustainable rural development, empowerment of women, prisoner rehabilitation, education for all, and environmental sustainability. The great achievement of Sri Sri Shankar is to mix and synergize the rich eastern traditions of Pranayaam, meditation, Bhajans and dance, with the established systematic training modules of the western traditions, leading to social spiritual and personality growth.

6.3.8 Dance and Music from Latin America

Latin dance is gaining great popularity all over the world as it involve partner dance. The popular dance forms are cha-cha-cha, rumba, samba, paso doble, etc. It also includes salsa, mambo, merengue, tumba, bachata, bomba, plena, and the Argentine tango. All major Indian cities have now caught us with the fire of these dances and many people are joining. This is a welcome trend. These dance forms are highly technical and provide great sense of enjoyment. Bachata is the most simple and effective dance form as it has regular 4 beat dance steps. In all these dance forms, the boy leads and the girl follows. The girl generally does most of the artistic body movements taking support of the boy. Salsa is the next most popular for with 123_567_ beats. The steps looks a little complicated at first, but is easy to learn. Learning dance make the body flexible. One would use hips, shoulder, body movements, turns, etc.

Jumba is the other popular dance form. This is pure rhythmic exercise done in group, led by a leader and is the individual version of the couple dances. Similar dance forms can be done with Bollywood style. Madhuri Dixit and others Bollywood has provided such nice lessons in YouTube. In all these dance forms, the beats and back ground music may be different, but the all body movement and exercise is almost similar. These dances when performed at individual level, bring flexibility and strength in body. One may club weight training and yoga with it. When done on the floor, the dance imbibes great social values. Since you dance with different partners, you learn to respect other people space and personality and this also provides stress-buster in life.

6.4   Dancercise with Madhuri Dixit

Dancercise[4] is a new term explained beautifully by leading Indian actress Madhuri Dixit. She asserts that dance is nothing but a series of exercise done with rhythm and theme. Jumba or Bollywood dances are much similar in spirit and nature. Efforts to make it artistic take it to a different plane. Perfection is not important but movement of each and every part of the body is important. Regular practise of these dance–steps will be much beneficial for our health. But it should be practiced under a trained guide. The dance requires warm up/cool down stages as well as stretching and strength training. With everyday practice, strength stamina and endurance will develop. The rhythm of musical beats with these steps makes it more interesting. Singing loudly and dancing without any inhibition is a therapy in itself.

6.5   Sexual Bias in Dance

In India, dance is often seen as an area of interest and participation for girls and only a few interested boys participate in dance. This is not true in tribal, African or Latin dances, where boys participate equally making the body of the boys strong and flexible. Most of the dance forms evolved in such a way that boys and girls complement each other. Stronger boys support naturally soft, light and flexible bodies of the girls. Most dance forms are based on balance of body weight connected between the boy and girl. Hence, it is strongly suggested that boys of India understand the importance of dance and start dancing. Sports, dance and music are taken as an integral part of the entertainment process.

6.6   Drum Circles and its Culture

"Drum Circle" is another innovation in the free expression of rhythms of music in dedicated group settings. It had its origin in late 1960s and early 1970s among informal counter-culture groups, which showed some Pan-African influences. It simply consists of groups of people, who gather informally, to play music together. The terms "drum jam" or "jam session" are also used to describe

it. The settings depends upon participants choices and may include courtyards, beaches, parks, concert parking lots, festivals, and retreats. The music is improvised and co-created by the participants and it may be or may not be open to the public, but the music is always a group expression [5-9].

It is not directed by and one person or sub-group or subscribe to any genre of instrumentation. It is a community oriented music circle, in a public and informal setup; its unique feature being improvised music created by group interactions. There is no music conductor or leader, but there may be facilitator or moderator to manage the uniform beats and goads all to participate. The prime instruments are drums and percussion, but may include other instruments, such as flutes or anything that can be banged on to make noise can be used as a percussion instrument such as cans, buckets, pipes, etc. It is great to see participants generating music together with their own listening and playing skills. Their participation is voluntary and often includes drumming, singing or chanting, dancing, and listening.

In 1991, during testimony before the **United States Senate Special Committee on Aging, Grateful Dead drummer Mickey Hart** stated:

> *"Typically, people gather to drum in drum "circles" with others from the surrounding community. The drum circle offers equality because there is no head or tail. It includes people of all ages. The main objective is to share rhythm and get in tune with each other and themselves, to form a group consciousness; to entrain and resonate. By entrainment, I mean that a new voice, a collective voice, emerges from the group as they drum together.[6]"*

Delhi Drum Circle [10]/ Noida Drummers: The author had first-hand experience of rhythm, dance music and spontaneous masti, when one fine morning he walked down the Deer Park, next to Hauz Khas Village, New Delhi and found it vibrating with sounds of percussion drums and various other musical instruments played by a group of Delhi Drum Circle enthusiasts. As he got nearer, he was welcomed by the beats, which lead him to a group of people in a circle, engrossed in playing their respective instruments. This circle met every alternate Sunday. Most of them carry a djembe (a western-African drum), some dhols and other musical instruments including saxophone, guitar, xylophone, flute, etc. [7]

One of the active members of the group wrote in the face book that, he had been to two drum jams sessions at Central Park, New York and found no difference in the attitude in Delhi and New York. They play seriously and no masti in-between playing. Lot of tourists come and start dancing. Whosoever is passing near the jam starts dancing and clicking pictures.

These are an open group of drummers in Delhi/Noida (a Suburban town of Delhi) consists of Sales & Marketing people, teachers, housewives, teachers, pilots, Doctors, Entrepreneurs etc., who not only meet for community drumming but also play the djembe drums to beat away stress and for the medical benefits of the drumming. Drumming is not only a good exercise for the human body and brain, but is also a good stress buster. It is an exercise of hands, arms & muscles and it also helps in keeping the mind alert and adaptable. It makes you a good listener, as one can play in harmony and improvise only if he/she is a good listener. As a group activity it also binds people & builds relationships. The people who come in for the drumming come as strangers but leave as friends.

Noida Drummers has gone a step further in their endeavour. Looking at the medical benefits of the drumming, they have started playing at the Orphanages, old age homes and for patients of chronic illnesses. Noida Drummers not only plays there but encourages onlookers to come forward and play drums with them, so that they can also be benefitted by the healing qualities of the drums. Drumming helps in healing disorders like stress disorders, psychological disorders, substance abusers, depression, personality disorders, strokes, Parkinson, High blood pressure, autistic & Alzheimer patients.

African Drumming: African drumming originated from religious festival celebration, very similar to Indian Makar Sankranti; as mingling of music and dance. A lot of African rhythms represent the culture and the rich history of the Malinke people. These rhythms represent specific events: a good harvest, grinding grain by hand, rites of passage, battles, freedom. It brings a community together. Hence, the African Master drummers don't respect modern drum circles, because there is no acknowledgment of their history or their people!

Conclusion: The author acknowledges that Drum Circles is a great expression of group music. The core group of drummers are addicted to the sound of drums. Where ever they play drums, they attract crowds. The drummers usually seat in circles and the people dance in between. The euphoria of dance cannot be expressed without attending such parties.

6.7   Music and Dance for Street Children

It is very sad to see children fighting for their life and dignity, working and loitering in the streets of cities. No system or law is able to eliminate the problems of street children and remove them permanently from their sufferings. They are not interested in the modern public education and our schools are not able to retain them. The pertinent question is - can we attract these young people to sing and dance, and perform to generate self-sustainability. This way, they will be part of entertainment business and also possibly do some studies.

Initially, what is needed is to identify and induct some good musicians to play on the streets on trial basis and analyse the reaction. We will interact with them and find out if these children, including the adults, are interested in such activities. Obviously, till self-sustainability comes with government support, we need to support them financially to take care of their basic needs. This is discussed further in an independent chapter.

6.8   Discussion

Even though it is clear that India has contributed to dance and music from ages, people enjoy hearing song and rarely participate in group music or dance in regular life, with a few exceptions. Drumming groups, Latin American and Bollywood dance groups are trying their best to gather momentum. The lack of interest and appreciation, lack of infrastructure where large groups can gather is lacking.

This lack of exposure and opportunity among Indians to enjoy group music, song and dance is very sad. This can be attributed to the fact that music and dance teachers are used to resort to highly complex and long form of teaching methods to teach the children. Most of the times, we learn music in small groups. As a result, the quality in improvement is low and rate of dropout is high.

Hence, this requires us to do some introspection and will to understand the importance of group activities including dance and music. In addition to external parks, each society should technically have a common venue with wooden floor where dance, music and indoor games can be enjoyed. A socio-economic model has to be evolved in a financially sustainable way.

6.9   Need for Research

The main purpose is to establish these entertainment forms as medium, to satisfy the socialization needs of the people by the way of mass participation. It also feels that we need to make simplistic tools in which children and all people can express themselves through writing their own songs and music. To satisfy these we would take the following steps:

a) Review in India by identifying, visiting and understanding how religious and cultural groups like Hare Krishna, Art of Living, Osho, Sai Baba, Sufi and Church choir-groups; are able to satisfy the socialization needs. It is proposed to carry out a survey, based on pre-defined formats, to evaluate their contributions.

b) Review of the existing music culture and mass participation in different countries.

c) Literature review of the above matter in books and journals.

d) Create an initial write up for its distribution in academic people, media, musicians, dancers and other performers and explore if these forms of entertainment can be used to create forums to satisfy the socialization needs.

e) Experimental studies and research with small groups to test our hypothesis.

f) Empower people to create songs: Make simple modules of musical notes, representing proper emotions and ask children and other people to try to express their feelings and attempt to write single or a few lines. These feelings and lines can then be compiled, categorized and utilized to create songs. By this way, can we empower children and all people of the society to express their inner feelings through writing songs and creating music by simple modules? If we cannot empower people to write songs, how do we expect a selected few to represent their true voice?

g) Street Children:

   i.   Trial experiment: Carry out trial experiment to see the reaction of street children to our dance and music formats and examine and explore their interest.

Let us Dance to the Sound of Music
Without bothering how good we are,

Let us make life in
Music and Dance

Just move your Body
And be Healthy and Happy

ii.   Interact with society: Create facilities in some schools, where these children can be taken during school hours, train them in these entertainment forms, and create ways to earn to make them self-sustainable. It is expected that when they enjoy their dignified life, they would also study like other children.

This write up explains a hypothesis that mass participation in music, song and dance would satisfy a greater need of social interaction and bridge the mental gaps that exists in most sections of people in India. While this form of mass entertainment is utilized mostly by religious groups in India, in other countries this is practiced in a socially accepted form. This chapter hopes to ignite a discussion where people and government act to slowly establish traditions of mass music and dance.

References

1. http://en.wikipedia.org/wiki/International_Society_for_Krishna_Consciousness

2. http://en.wikipedia.org/wiki/Chaitanya_Mahaprabhu

3. http://www.artofliving.org/art-living-overview

4. https://www.youtube.com/watch?v=czRo4YiVmAw

5. http://en.wikipedia.org/wiki/Drum_circle

6. The Healing Power of the Drum, by Robert Lawrence Friedman, MA.

7. https://www.mickeyhart.net/bio?destination=Pages/senspeech.html, Rhythm As A Tool For Healing and Health in The Aging process,

8. Finding Sanctuary in Nature: Simple Ceremonies in the Native American Tradition for Healing Yourself and Others, by Jim Path Finder Ewing (Nvnehi Awatisgi), Findhorn Press, Scotland, 2007.

9. Freestyle Community Drum Circles, by Rick Cormier.

10. http://www.sodelhi.com/communities-clubs/delhi-drum-circle-hauz-khas-new-delhi

Music & Dance
for Street Children

CHAPTER 7
MUSIC AND DANCE FOR STREET CHILDREN

7.1   Introduction

Street children are an everyday sight in the metro cities of India for most of us. At traffic intersections, they knock on car windows seeking money or food. In busy market places, they try to get your attention by simply asking for money or food that you

> *There is need to explore the possibility of enriching the life of street children through music and entertainment.*

are eating. Some of them are under adult supervision or with their families, while some are alone and living independent lives. They try to impress the wealthy looking foreigners more with the hope of getting bigger money. However, not all street children survive on begging. A lot of them work hard to earn money, either for themselves as individuals or as contribution to their families. The Indian society in general, and governments and law enforcement agencies in particular, have looked down upon street children as a part of various social problems like poverty and illiteracy that plague us. Street children are also considered as one of the most visible forms of urban poverty.

> *Every time I see street children,*
> *My heart cries.*
>
> *I wonder,*
> *Can't we all sing and dance together,*
>
> *And provide them a reason*
> *To live?*

Why are these children on the streets? What can be done to remove these children from streets? Various organizations and governments bodies have attempted several ways but they have not succeeded. Although a lot of research has been done on the street children, both nationally and internationally, most of the work attempts to enrich them by making them work in factories, providing the vocational training. All these approaches are ways that provide minimal income and require these children to calm. These children often return to the street as they provide them the freedom and also allow them to earn.

This chapter presents the possibility of enriching the street children through music and entertainment along with the review of past work done in India and abroad. Next, it presents a systematic plan where initial experimental plan and future course of actions are explained.

It is the author's hypothesis that if we can empower them in such a way that these children can earn with respect, the desired results can be achieved. One may note that many people have tried this approach but have failed earlier. So, the author feels that empowerment has to be interesting and able to capture their energy and skills and provide them high respect. Possibly, music and dance are the factors through which we can attract these children so that they become entertainers and become financially independent. The children should be taken away from parents if necessary for fixed period of time and returned to their parents at night. Compensation can be given as these children start concentrating on entertainment. As they are removed from street, provided good food, they might be attracted to receive informal education also.

The attempt to make this children work as entertainer may look like violation of some basic rights, the

Life's a dance you learn as you go,
Sometimes you lead, sometimes you follow,
Don't worry about what you don't know,
Life's a dance you learn as you go.

Song by John Michael Montgomery

author feels optimistic that society and law will permit this as an experiment as all other approaches to remove them from streets and providing education have failed. In this approach, at least the children may learn informally and are removed from the streets.

7.2   Earlier Studies on the Street Children in India

Street children are found mostly in large cities of the developing countries. It is claimed that India alone has the largest population of street children the world. Child Line India explains that UNICEF in 2003 mentioned 100 million street children worldwide. However, this figure is not based on actual survey studies. In 1994, UNICEF estimated 11 million street children in India. This it seems is a drastic underestimation. Another estimate stated 3.15 lakhs street children in cities like Mumbai, Kolkata, Madras, Kanpur, Bangalore and Hydrabad and around 1 lakh street children in Delhi. Internationally, efforts have been put by UNICEF to understand the conditions of the street children and intervene with suitable measures.

According to UNICEF(1986), street children fall under three groups depending upon the degree of family support. The first group has been called "Candidates for the street", where the children live with their families. The second group has been called "Children on the street" where the children have some contact with their families but that is inadequate and sporadic. The third group has been called "Children of the street" where the children do not have any family connection and live independently. UNICEF has also identified three broad approaches which may be useful in improving the lives of the street children. The first uses legal instruments to prevent or reduce the exploitation by adopting new regulations and enforcing those which already exist; the second seeks to provide basic services in order to help them develop; and the third one seeks to enrich and humanize the street children by forging a link between work and education.

In India, a number of city specific studies have been done around the street children. Patel documented the ways the street children meet their daily needs in Bombay (now Mumbai) (Patel, 1990). In Kanpur, an exploratory study conducted by Pandey (1993) revealed the problems faced by the street children including absence of guidance on tackling life, exposure to polluted environment and rough weather. Similar situational analyses and studies have been done in Bombay (D'Lima & Gosalia, 1992), Indore (Phillips, 1992), Calcutta (now Kolkata) (Ghosh, 1992), Bangalore (now Bengaluru, Reddy 1992), Madras (now Chennai) (Arimpoor, 1992), Delhi (Paniker & Desai, 1992) and Noida (Sekar, 2004). Mathur et. al. examined the incidence and intensity of abuse in five areas namely "general abuse", "health abuse", "verbal abuse", "physical abuse" and "psychological abuse" in street children in Jaipur (Mathur et. al., 2009, also Mathur, 2009). In another work, a street child's experience with vocational education in Kolkata has been studied within the historical context of colonial education policies (Balagopalan, 2002). The lives of the girls on streets in Delhi were explored in a study spanning four countries, the results of which indicated that such girls were most likely to get involved in antisocial activities with companions, had low problem solving abilities, and had more chances of getting into depression and mental health related problems (Sharma & Verma, 2013).

In yet another study, the authors found that the predominant reasons behind children being on streets include "family discord", "domestic abuse," "abandonment," "eviction," and "poverty-driven prostitution" (Mitra & Deb, 2004). Moreover, the working conditions for most of them pose great risks on their health, especially the waste-pickers as found in a study on waste-pickers in Bengaluru (Hunt, 1996). Kombarakan conducted an in-depth study of the street children in Mumbai and concluded that such children are there in urban centres because of the underlying structural causes like rural poverty; and that their stress management abilities must be acknowledged first before providing them support services (Kombarakan, 2004).

A couple of studies have pointed out that a faulty education system could be one of the reasons behind this problem. It has been argued that a schooling system that delivers poor quality education and is oppressive and discriminatory for many, the system itself becomes counter-productive (Raman, 2000). Another study points out that the focus of the Indian education system is narrow and is always questioning the ability of the students rather than questioning the teaching methodology or the curriculum (Singal, 2006). These are indirect observations, yet important because the connection between childhood and education is extremely critical for the overall development of the children.

The past literature on street children in India suggests many areas which are under-researched. Experiments towards their empowerment, especially using tools such as music and dance, are one of such areas where the research is almost non-existent. The present work seeks to fill that gap.

7.3   Earlier Studies on the Street Children outside India

This issue has received considerable attention in other countries as well. A study on China's policy on the street children evaluated the effectiveness of the government managed Protection and Education Centre for Street Children (PEC) programme. It concluded by showing the poor performance of the programme because it did not allow the street children to participate in the decision making process regarding their future.

The street children in Shanghai preferred the streets over the comforts given in the PEC because they did not want to compromise on their freedom and resisted forced reunion with unsupportive parents (Lam & Cheng, 2008). Tyler et al. (1987)

conducted study in Bogota, Colombia, where they found that these children were living their lives without control of adults and were acquiring a diverse set of skills. Woan et al. (2012) systematically reviewed the literature on the health status of street children and youth in low and middle income countries in which they summarized the demographic data and structural factors associated with street life. The review found that adverse conditions of living in streets resulted into many ill effects on the physical and psychological well-being of the street children.

Turnbull et al. (2009) analyzed the interactions of the street children with their helpers and service providers in Mexico City. While documenting their frustrations with getting the street children to cooperate with the research objectives, they concluded by asking the helpers to understand their contribution to the problem; and becoming more aware of their influence on the identity of each child. Kerfoot et al. (2007) reported the backgrounds and physical and emotional well-being of street children in Kiev, Ukraine. The authors concluded that different approaches must be developed to solve this problem as street children present different variety of vulnerabilities.

7.4 Themes for Intervention

Broadly speaking, there are two themes for intervention. One is music and the other one is dance. The former includes songs, instruments and lyrics. The later includes rhythmic physical expression and movements of the body as per the music. The two may be combined to be called entertainment from our perspective. All the efforts of the group will revolve around these two themes. Experiments will be done to see their effect on the street children.

For example, the street children will be exposed to impromptu music on the street and then their reaction and response will be observed, recorded and documented. Similarly, their willingness and aptitude to learn music and dance will be thoroughly studied and used in the experiments proposed by the author.

7.5   Proposal

This project involves a number of activities which must be accomplished satisfactorily for its overall success. For the sake of convenience, the project has been broken down in to small action points. These have been explained as under:

a.   **Look for Guides and Ph.D. students**

The group will approach a number of universities and institutions of higher education to explore the possibility of finding Guide(s) who are willing to supervise the research at Master's and Doctoral levels on various topics that will emerge from the project. Such topics will be finalized through mutual consultations between the institution and the group.

b.   **Look for a dedicated musician**

The group will also hire a dedicated musician with practical knowledge of conducting live music shows. This will enable the group to conduct musical events for street children at a number of places.

c.   **Trial experiments with or without guides and Ph.D. students**

Ideally, the project will start with some guides and Ph.D. students. However, in case the guides and Ph.D. students are not found, trial experiment will be done using dedicated musician. The following will be the areas where the researchers will focus:

i.   Response of street children to learn music and dance.

ii.   Study the family background and life of interested children.

iii.   Ask the parents if they would provide the children for 8 hours for vocational education, dance and music to create self-sustainable independent life.

d. **Look for a school to conduct the experiment**

Quite obviously, the agenda of research is a serious one and can't be done right away at anywhere. A place has to be identified for conducting a number of experiments. The group sincerely feels that a school should be the ideal place for this objective. Thus, the group will approach a number of schools with the concept and list of activities/experiments

e. **Food and monetary compensation may be necessary**

It is felt that providing food and monetary compensation to the participating street children may be necessary because most of them work for food and money. If we want them to do something different from what they have been doing, food and monetary compensation must be offered.

f. **Approach government and private bodies for funding of the project**

The group cannot sustain this vital project on its own. Eventually, the government and other private bodies will be approached for funding the project which is going to be a project of national importance.

g. **Photography/videography and documentary details to be maintained.**

From the perspectives of research as well as the long term goals of the project, it is very important to record and document all the activities which will be done with the street children. This will include still photography, videography, observatory remarks and interviews. It shall be the group's endeavour to create high quality content which may be shown to the outside world using media like internet and television. This will create the maximum impact.

7.6 Conclusion

The problem of street children presents a unique challenge to the current social system. It seems that only a child centric economic empowerment strategy will work towards betterment of their condition. Music and dance have the potential to bring such children out of the streets.

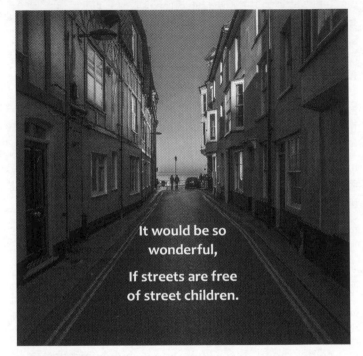

It would be so wonderful,

If streets are free of street children.

References

1. http://www.childlineindia.org.in/street-children-india.htm (15/4/2015)

2. http://www.unicef.org/evaldatabase/files/ZIM_01-805.pdf (UNICEF, 1986)

3. Patel S. (1990), Street Children, hotel boys and children of pavement dwellers and construction workers in Bombay - how they meet their daily needs, „Environment and Urbanization" 2(2), p.11

4. Rajendra Pandey(1993), Street children of Kanpur : a situational analysis / study, Noida : National Labour Institute, Child Labour Cell, 1993

5. D'Lima and Gosalia, R. (1992) Street children of Bombay: A situational analysis. Child Labour Series, National Labour Institute, Noida.

6. W. S. K. Phillips, Street Children of Indore: A Situational Analysis, National Labour Institute, Child Labour Cell, 1992 - Street children - 127 pages

7. Ghosh A (1992), Street Children of Calcutta, National Labour Institute, Child Labour cell, NOIDA, p. 14

8. Reddy MSN (1992): National Labour Institute "Street Children of Bangalore", Child labour cell, NOIDA; p 3-4.

9. Arimpoor, J. (1992) Street children of Madras: A situational analysis. National Labour Institute, Noida.

10. Paniker, R. and Desai, K. (1992), "Street Girls of Delhi: Case Studies", Child Labour Cell, VV Giri National Labour Institute, Noida

11. Sekar, H. R. (2004), "Child Labour in Urban Informal Sector: A Study of Ragpickers in Noida", VV Giri National Labour Institute, Noida

12. Desai (1995), Physical abuse, sexual victimization and illicit drug use replication of structural analysis among a new sample of High-Risk youths, Violence and victims, Vol. 4, No.2.

13. Meena Mathur ; Prachi Rathore ; Monika Mathur (2009), Incidence, type and intensity of abuse in street children in India. Child Abuse & Neglect Volume:33 Issue:12 Dated:December 2009 Pages:907 to 913

14. Meena Mathur(2009), Socialization of Street Children in India -A Socio-economic Profile, Psychology Developing Societies, vol. 21, p. 2299-325.

15. Balagopalan, S (2002) Constructing indigenous childhoods: Colonialism, vocational education and the working child. Childhood 9: pp. 20-34

16. Kathakali Mitra and Sibnath Deb (2002), Stories of street children: Findings from a field study, Social Change : December 2004 : Vol. 34 No. 4, p. 77-85.

17. Caroline Hunt (1996), Child waste pickers in India: the occupation and its health risks, Environment and Urbanization, Vol. 8, No. 2, October 1996, p. 111-118

18. Kombarakaran, F.A. (2004), Street children of Bombay: their stresses and strategies of coping, Children and Youth Services Review 26, p.867

19. Raman, V "The Politics of Childhood" in My Name is Today: A Dossier on Children and Children's Rights; Children and Development Issues, Vol 1, preface, 2003

20. Singal, N. (2006a). Inclusive education in India: international concept, national interpretation. International Journal of Disability, Development and Education, 53 (3), 351-369.

21. Tyler, F., Holliday, M., Tyler, S., Echeverry, J., & Zea, M. (1987). Street children and play. Children's Environmental Quarterly, 4, 13-17

22. Woan, J., Lin, J. & Auerswald, C. (2013). The health status of street children and youth in low- and middle-income countries. Journal of Adolescent Health, 53(3), 314–321.e12.

23. Turnbull, Bernardo & Hernández, Raquel & Reyes, Miguel (2009). Street children and their helpers; an actor-oriented approach. Children and youth services review, 31, 1283-1288

24. Kerfoot M, Koshyl V, Roganov O, Mikhailichenko K, Gorbova I, Pottage D. (2007), The health and well-being of neglected, abused and exploited children: the Kyiv Street Children Project. Child Abuse Negl. 2007 Jan;31(1):27-37. 2007 Jan 17.

Counselling

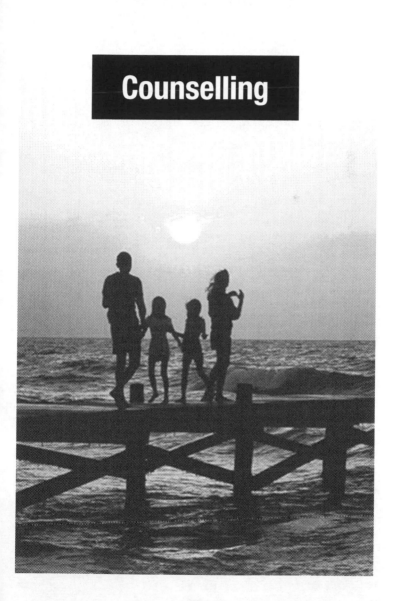

CHAPTER 8
COUNSELLING

8.1 Introduction

Counselling is a much misinterpreted and misunderstood term in the Indian context and has been considered as sign of weakness on the part of the mentally vulnerable, weak and ill persons. The stigmas attached with this supportive and helping services, are very strong in the Indian society. Counselling is a helping tool for a person in indecisive, disturbed, incongruent stage and stress needs guidance support and psychological help from a trained volunteer or counsellor.

Psychological Counselling brings positive changes in the thought process during crisis period.

In past, Family-Guru performed this thankless duty.

In more problematic stage, one may require medical help too from a professional psychiatrist, depending on the situation. In some situation, Counselling is lifesaving. There is one more form of counselling where the people are made aware of the laws, feeling and rights of other people, realities of life, so that he can take correct action and create a better world.

The background of this chapter is rooted in the real story and experiences of the author. The author had varied and different experiences of childhood problems, similar to many ADHD (Attention Deficit Hyperactivity Disorder) people; yet he was lucky to enjoy repeated successes in his life. Though, he failed in various literature based subjects in school or showed learning disorder, his progress in life was not disturbed since he was showered with love and support from the people around him. His talent was manifested in science-based subjects. It was apparent that he had a fantastic analytical mind that was reflected in his deep understanding in maths and physics. The key to his success was having a clear objective in each step of his life. He pioneered his own methods and process of solving life problems.

He once underwent a stage, where he dreamt of his son, becoming an Olympian at age of 16 year; also getting him 325 JEE-IIT All India rank, at age of 18 years and also becoming a medallist in Olympics at age of 20 years. It was an impossible and over-ambitious dream, which tore him apart, as he faced his first major defeat in his life. The concept elaborated in this book is a direct result of the failures, and his keen observations, as he witnessed various deficiencies of the thinking and cultural pattern of Indian society.

His experience in Japan helped him to understand many life problems and our inability to cope up with them. He himself was cornered by various personal problems and was overwhelmed by the extreme stress level due to family conflicts. Finally, he underwent Counselling, which made him realise the importance of mind control, coping and adjustment skills, under the guidance of Personal Counsellor and Life Coach, Mr. Prakash Chandra. Within 2 years of the counselling, amazing results were achieved in the field of adjustment and coping up with stress. This chapter has been written in collaboration of Dr. Supratic Gupta with Mr. Prakash Chandra, Professional Counsellor, for highlighting the importance of mental health, adjustment, coping skills, stress management, information (legal and general) and mind/anger control.

8.2　Concept

This chapter aims to present in concise way, the thoughts and experiences of Dr. Supratic Gupta and Prakash Chandra in starting counselling services, focussing on some of the priority areas and to highlight the steps that will be taken in this field in a financially viable way. It is based on the author's unique life experiences and also their analysis of the pressing problems of different age groups.

The purpose is to initiate discussions among teachers, psychologists, academicians, and media on the specific ideas on counselling presented and give their inputs, on how to conduct researches and create counselling modules and models, after testing the hypotheses presented here. It should lead to popularise and to create various fora to satisfy the counselling needs of society. The aim is also to identify the types of services, to be provided to the targeted groups, in a business based sustainable models.

8.3   Pre-birth and Post-birth Counselling

It is very important to consider children as national assets of the country. One must realize that the human brain starts developing in the mother's womb, as it is depicted in the mythological story of Abhimanyu story in Mahabharata. Many experiments have shown good responses of foetus to the external sound and touch stimuli. So, it is imperative that the expectant mother and father should be made aware and trained in the developmental aspects of the foetus, which prevent the pre-birth complication and insure healthy growth. Similarly, the parents should also be made aware of all the aspects of the developmental growth of the infant baby after the birth. Proper knowledge must be disseminated on the vaccination, diet and the exercises parts to the parents, for maintaining the proper physical and mental growth of the foetus. The proposed counselling services will cover both aspects by providing a counselling service by trained volunteers and professionals.

Japan has a tradition of making the first time mothers aware of the above problems and impart them training in pre-birth as well as post-birth processes, with the supportive help of health care professional and volunteer ladies. It covers all the aspects of child care including- baby bath, changing nappies, diet, hygiene, breast feeding, and feeding. The expectant mother is also explained the process of child-birth such as, identifying the signs and frequency of contraction and relaxation during the time of child birth and trained how to put pressure on the womb, deep breathing and exhale of breath with a sound. If the mother follows these instructions, the process of childbirth becomes easier and less painful.

Japan has also evolved an excellent system of post-birth counselling. The Japanese medical system creates a personal book/ file of each child, from the time of conception to the age of 3 years. In this book, the complete health records and personal developmental details of the baby and mother from conception to birth and post birth, are maintained, which includes, weight, height, dental development, diet, vaccinations, which are recorded meticulously.

Apart from the medical services in Japan, the city-officers organisers organize parallel health care services, where a group of volunteers make regular visits to the expectant mothers and advise the mothers on the post-birth care of their children and themselves. These volunteers are usually the mothers, whose children have left home and they are sitting idle, having no job responsibilities. This is an excellent way of engaging this group of women who has experience of child birth in a mutually beneficial way. Their engagement keeps in a good mental health also. There is a working effective system to monitor and record these activities.

The authors propose to raise awareness on the above Japanese experiences and will facilitate further research on these areas by experts and policy makers. The purpose is to find out how to implement these practices in Indian situations. The authors are not specialists in this field, hence proper research will have to be conducted to create relevant training modules for both pre-birth and post birth period for the mothers.

The modules may be made by adapting the Japanese experiences and may be modified to suit Indian conditions. Currently, Indian health professional, including nurses and Asha workers under NRHM are provided training in pre-natal and post –natal care, but the quality of the services has left much more room for improvement.

We will initiate discussion and projects to design new training modules, which are upgraded and improved further, after taking into consideration the experience of other countries like Japan and USA, keeping in mind the local conditions in Indian cities and villages. The proposed counselling services will cover the above mentioned aspects by providing a counselling service by trained volunteers and professionals.

The proposed counselling model will cover these three aspects of counselling:

a. **Knowledge about biological and food requirements**

   • Diet and Nutrition: Proper Diet and Nutrition for the optimum development of the baby and keeping the health of the mother is the primary focus.

   • Breast Feeding: Develop understanding on topics of breast milk as the complete food, ideal feeding positions, common problems faced and remedies, breast v/s bottle feeding, feeding interval, etc.

   • Labour and Delivery: The birth preparation sessions taking through the different types of deliveries, how to identify pre-labour and labour signs, contractions/ relaxations and symptoms, tricks to ease labour pains, breathing exercises with sound, labour positions, etc.

b. **Exercise, hygiene and related topics**

   • Pre-natal group exercise class covering all relevant exercises and breathing techniques and prepares mother for the labour.

- Post Natal Exercises introduced to bring mother muscles back to the pre-pregnancy tone and this is best achieved with a post-natal routine.

- Infant Care: It will cover common new born concerns of holding, handling the baby, bathing techniques, diapers v/s nappies, baby massage, play in water, etc.

c. Psychological and family counselling and support

- Dispel myths and attitudes surviving around pregnancy, gender of the expected baby and fears about delivery.

- Provide information to pregnant women, their spouses and other family members enhancing family adjustments.

- Birth techniques processes and changes in body will be elaborated in facilitating their delivery process

- To enhance their coping skills in building further resistance towards their pain and torment on the course of pregnancy though coping techniques

- Post Natal Care & Recovery covering the changes a woman's body goes through during and post child birth and how she can help herself attain recovery in the optimum way.

8.4   Adolescent Counselling

Gender sensitization of boys and girls: It is suggested that in adolescent counselling services, there should be sex sensitization of the boys and girls at an early age. In India, the girls are mostly provided gender and sexual training by the mothers and other people around them, as girls undergo sea of changes in their bodies, affecting them psychologically. This is also done to avoid unwanted pregnancy and other complications. They are also trained about household chores, cooking etc. looking at the immediate future requirement in life. However, these training provided to them depends on what the mother understands and cannot be called as correct or scientific and in tandem with the current psychological thinking. In fact, what should be taught or not itself is a big topic of debate.

On the other hand, boys are not at all provided any training related to domestic chores like cooking. They are never provided any training for how to interact with opposite sex in a healthy way.

In reality, both boys and girls grow up with their distorted expectations from each other, creating a wide ranging problem in the society. All these problems can be minimized by evolving effective adolescent training modules. Irrespective of gender, children should be taught to take care of domestic chores, cooking and house management. Children should interact in joint counselling sessions, where both sex get opportunity to interact under guidance to understand various aspects of future life. This will also take care of gender sensitization, where boy and girls will become aware of body developments, psychological difference and also defuse the initial inquisitiveness about opposite sex creating a healthier and safer society.

One more important thing that requires attention is to explain the role of love, responsibility, compatibility such that children do not take decision in a state of

> Boys should be trained to be more gender sensitive towards girls.

hurry or under the hypnotic effect of first love. Children should be taught that compatibility between partners is important aspect of life and should be considered while choosing a partner. Openness, clarity and truthfulness are important in any relationship.

To give more emphasis, it is stated that boys in general require more counselling than girls, for a better and balanced society. It is suggested that the boys should be trained to be more gender sensitive towards girls in the family itself by the parents and elders. They should be made aware about girl's physical moods fluctuations, occurring due to hormone, physical and psychological growth of girls at various ages. The counselling should be done in an interactive ways, so that their sexual awareness about other sex is not repressed. Their inquisitiveness and sexual question should not be brushed off. The parents should also be trained in these matters.

Similarly the girls should be sensitised regarding the boy sexuality, physical growth and what is good touch and bad touch. It will curb sexual harassment and rape mentality among the youth.

In a broader sense, even social issues like equality of sex, dowry, molestation and legal punishments for sexual crimes should be discussed freely without prejudgement. It will check and control many social evils and crimes.

8.5   Pre-Marital and Post- Marital Counselling

Marriage brings a sea of changes in the life. Two known or unknown, individuals and families are uniting such that needs of all are satisfied. It is impossible to summarize all possible scenarios as this depends on the society and financial status.

Hence, the author proposes development of general modules for the boys and girls, expecting to marry. It will take care of the problems of maladjustment and marital discords, which occurs after the marriages. They have to also learn about the relationship building skills and sexual compatibility issues. The matters mentioned hereafter are personal views of the authors and may require detailed research to establish the truth:

- It is assumed that the people taking pre-and post-marital sex would have already taken the gender sensitization counselling module, which had already made them aware about sexual uniqueness, equality and role issues. It will help both the sexes to be sensitive to each other.

- A sexual awareness module needs to be developed, which will explain to both sex participants, the various matters related to internal body mechanisms of women- egg formation, conception, menstruation cycle, mood changes and sexual mechanisms and processes of men- masturbation, sperm formation, sex myths, misconceptions etc.

- There should be specially designed home-making awareness modules, where both boys and girls should learn- how to share house hold works and support each other's, while respecting other's mutual works. It would be expected that responsibilities should be shared depending of roles and abilities of the individuals.

- There should be a series of life-skills modules, which would develop coping and adjustment skills among boys and girls going for marriages. This ranges from skills of communication, anger-control, self-introspection, ability to detect potential triggers for conflicts, negotiation and problem-solving skills.

Dr. Gupta has observed that many males, who had never been violent in their life, suddenly started resorting to aggressive and violent behaviour after marriage. It is important to do research and find out the possible

There should be a series of Life-skills, Home-making and Relationship-building modules, which would develop coping and adjustment skills among boys and girls going for marriages and make better adjusted families.

reasons underlying this onset of abusive and violent behaviour of males. It may be result of not knowing how to cope with opposite sex, and appropriate action need to be taken in such case. The males should be taught that being physically violent is not a legal option and have serious legal implications. This knowledge of law is not sufficient to deter violence.

But, if the other side continues to provoke, use 'touch-me-not' or sexual boycott as a weapon, anger control would be difficult as some time or other it is bound to erupt as a volcano. Hence, simultaneously, it should be counselled to women that having regular sex can in fact defuse tension between the couple. Showing affection to your partner in front of children are not unhealthy practices as these are natural things.

These are not exhaustive list and author expects a sincere research on these topic.

- Relationship needs skills, for making it successful. Marriage is one of the most intense relationship building exercises. There should be a series of Relationship Building modules, which will teach the boys and girls, how to develop human skills like- trust/ love, communication, sharing, transparency, relaxation and pro-activeness in taking life decisions.

- Co-dependency: It has been often seen that the male and female become the sole friend to each other, neglecting other social relations. They make sacrifices and cut off their enjoyable interests and activities. This over dependence leads to more problems. This should be strongly discouraged. Each should maintain cordial relationship with other friends and relatives, such that they do not depend on each other all the time. Proper personal space should be maintained otherwise this would lead to suffocation at later stage. One should not also sacrifice hobbies like dance, music etc. as later children would surely be more happy with parents with such hobbies.

• It is also assumed that these people should take the pre-post birth counselling as this will train them about matter pregnancy, health and development of the foetus in mother's womb and finally a healthy growth of the baby.

8.6   Midlife Counselling

Firstly, we have to understand the real meaning of Midlife crisis and correlate it with Indian context. The objective of Midlife counselling is develop coping skills among the middle aged persons to face the period of psychological stress and turmoil, due to specific condition. It aims to make people more aware so that they can navigate the middle age, in balanced and adjusting way. The meaning of Midlife Crisis (from Random House Dictionary of the English Language) is "A period of psychological stress (depression & anxiety) occurring in middle age, thought to be triggered by a physical, occupational, or domestic event, as menopause, diminution of physical prowess, job loss or departure of children from the home."

Midlife transitions, which affect both men and women, can also be difficult on our close friends, family, and partners. Sometimes, in an attempt to stave off feelings of grief or anxiety that can accompany maturity, people engage in what might be called "regression;" they may have an affair, buy a new car, stay out late, abuse drugs or alcohol, or otherwise try to recapture the exhilaration of youth. Irrational behaviour is common during mid-life and many otherwise level-headed

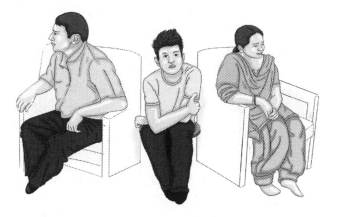

Mid-life Crisis is Normal

Professional Counselling is Important

people do things that seem completely out of character. Divorce, infidelity, financial irresponsibility, job change radical self-improvement and religious activities are some of the actions people take during this time.

The matters mentioned hereafter are personal views of the authors, a type of hypotheses and may require detailed research to establish the truth:

- After marriage, comes the entry of the children. The couple usually diverts all energy sacrificing most of their own happiness to bring up the child. Though this is not a healthy practice as it has been explained above, this is inevitable to some extent. As the child grows and leaves home for the purpose of studies or job, a typical problem has been noticed in both genders. This is more predominant among the urban sections of society with small families, as a void suddenly comes to the life. The midlife crisis is also hitting out the Indian middle age like hurricane, disturbing the peace of mind and the families all across.

- It has one more angle. It is the age, where women's sexuality is in a decline, where male sexuality is reinforced by the financial strength that he has in this stage of his life. It is very difficult to say what is right and what is wrong. Hence, author feels that the first and foremost thing that can be done is to document the various possible patterns and make short documentary movies such that we can make people aware of the arriving uncertainties.

- It is absolutely necessary to make use of a support network; individuals should discuss major life changes with their colleagues, friends, families, and professional counsellor and community volunteers.

Life of
Women and Happiness

CHAPTER 9
LIFE OF WOMEN AND HAPPINESS

9.1   Introduction

In the evolutionary growth of the human race, the subjugation of the women by male-dominated hierarchical society is the bitter truth. This outlook and attitude has divided the social order from the earliest human civilisation. Indian history is also full of many instances of male domination and sexual discrimination of women, right from the Vedic civilisation to the mediaeval ages and to post- modern age. Whether it is child marriage or Sati Pratha or shocking case of Nirbahaya rape recently, women empowerment, safety and sexuality issue has remained a blot on equality.

All the above mentioned issues invariably deal with shaping - what and how, women think and feel comfortable with. It also is linked with creating a just and happy society, where our children can grow up in a safe environment. No section of society can be happy with either side – men or women – feeling that justice is not being done on them.

To create a just society, there are two important things that needs action and introspection as it involve the future of our children:

- Shape how boys think and learn to face life.

- Try to understand how people around the world have tried to solve the matter of women's choice, freedom and safety.

In this chapter, author shares his experience and feelings about this society and expresses interest to start a project in search for answer to these questions.

We all come in different colours,
Colours make life beautiful.

Allow us to be what we are,
In a Free and Fair world,

To create a better world.

The views expressed in this chapter are not based on research but on personal experience and may not be true. Some of the statement may look like stereotype statements. These matters are discussed to trigger research, thought and discussion on these lines. The author apologises in advance if anyone is hurt by these statements.

9.2   The World from Women's Point of View

Statistically, as per Wikipedia, literacy in India is has grown to 74.04% (2011 figure) from 12% at the end of British rule in 1947. The level is well below the world average literacy rate of 84%, with 82.14% for men and 65.46% for women.

In most middle class families, the childhood usually starts in a good note for the girl. She is usually the attraction in the family and society. In school, the girls are on the average doing much better compared to boys in any field. This is possibly a way of nature to protect women. Puberty also comes to them almost 3 years before their male counterparts. In this sense, they are clearly 3 years ahead of the own class mates.

As they grow, they face various challenges. Sexuality and their inner emotions often play havoc on their psychological existence. Often they fall in love with people in uncontrolled and infatuated manner, even though it may not be logical. These children overcome all these stages of life gaining complicated experience to make them mature. Good and bad are difficult terms

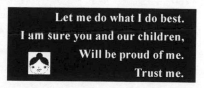

Let me do what I do best.
I am sure you and our children,
Will be proud of me.
Trust me.

Why do you expect me to Cook?
Do I know how to take of the Child?
Did I get any special Training?

Outsource these Duties.
Let me be what I want to be.
Empower me.
Free me.

Ref: Japanese Culture of
Hoikuen and Shokudo

to define any of these experiences. How they face the world, is often dependent on the cultural background.

In India, sexuality is rarely discussed. NCERT and academic researches has analysed it in details and also suggested many steps to make the children aware about these issues, through classroom training and modern curriculum. The sexual topics are complex and attached with social stigmas, so they are discussed in cursory manners by the teachers and the parents, who have little understanding and training on them. They deal with the sexuality issues of the teens in the outmoded and traditional way. This problem is in fact worse for boys, since the teachers and parents avoid discussion.

Women sexuality starts after puberty. The chemical reactions and preparation of her body for motherhood starts at 13-15 years. In earlier times, women were married early and attained motherhood in early age. Increase in the marriage and child-bearing age has been a modern phenomenon in human history. This is more particularly true in cities and educated middle class. The correctness of this decision will be judged by the future. This leads to wondering whether we should fully or partially suppress sexuality till marriage. Does suppression of the sexuality not affect the growth of the body? Do lack of dance, music, entertainment and exercise affect the healthy growth? Hence, it is important to study how sexuality is handled across the world and do deep introspection to find out the appropriate way to handle it in Indian context. Do these things have any relationship with the increasing trend of sexual violence that we see in our society in India today?

The girls, in class X and XII, do very well compared to boys. However, their career choice is a tough and complicated question as they logically wish to settle down faster compared to boys. These are difficult questions with no easy answers. Beyonce Knowles speaks her mind out when she asserts that the earning power of women is an important criterion for gender equality. But this is not an easy question, as motherhood puts them on a difficult choice. In reality of India, after completion of the education both boys and girls get sucked into adult life of marriage, motherhood and ... well, when do they actually live their life? Most women have to leave job to take care of children and their rearing.

The working women have to carry out double burden - carry out the job responsibility and also do the home chores, from washing clothes to cooking food. If a couple decides not to cook food at home, there is no healthy food option available in India. Motherhood cannot be compromised. Delayed motherhood creates complications. It is not just the childbirth, it is the anxiety of how the child grows that keeps the women from work place. Japan has an excellent facility called Hoikuen where children are placed in experienced hand with best infrastructure so that the children can grow normally.

Cooking food is another difficult area for working ladies. Food available outside is often more tasty but not healthy. Japan has a system called Shokudo, where food is cooked in various categories – soup, salad, main course, deserts, etc. Each day a separate but limited number of choices are available.

> *You know, equality is a myth, and for some reason, everyone accepts the fact that women don't make as much money as men do. I don't understand that. Why do we have to take a backseat? I truly believe that women should be financially independent from their men.*
>
> *And let us face it, money gives men the power to run the show. It gives men the power to define value. They define what is sexy. And men define what's feminine.*
>
> *It is ridiculous.*
>
>   -   *Beyonce Knowles.*

One cannot order separately, but have to choose among the few available choices. Author have seen this type of facility implemented even in German University canteen. Since food is not wasted, it is cheaper. Since the food is predetermined, you waste less time and are served warm. There is a segment of food shop that satisfies the breakfast, and other food option to the elderly people. There are also food shops, where just one menu is served each day, it is homely and cheap. This type of food facilities should be implemented in all housing colonies, freeing the women to work on their strength and likings. In other words, community kitchen facility should be encouraged.

Fun and enjoyment are rare for women and gossiping is the only option available for many. Though the culture of dance and music is slowly getting acceptance in India, this is rare. If one talk about health and flexibility of Indian women, they are conscious. They start yoga starting often from middle age. This is a very important area that requires deep introspection.

The proposed cross-cultural comparative study is to mirror all these sentiments directly from the eyes of the women from across the world. This will act a good starting point of research also.

9.3 The World from Men's Point of View

The delayed puberty in boys starting from 14-18 years age allow them a relaxed childhood. By this time, their girl class mates have already reached maturity due to early puberty. Boys usually spend more time in games and exercise. But as they reach their puberty from age 15-18 (Class IX-XII – four years), they are often forced to leave all games and exercise and concentrate in studies. It becomes a matter of pride, if you are a good student to get through national level competitions like IIT or Medical entrance. Their personal choice rarely matters, as they have not been exposed to the world and the career choices. They are groping in dark about their aims in life. It is in this regards, educational portal is proposed so that children can learn about pros and cons of various educational possibilities and make a proper career decision in life.

Male sexuality grows similarly in unawareness. Self-experimentation, masturbation and secretly watching easily available distorted adult films through internet- usually forms the basis of sexual knowledge. They are rarely taught how to interact, talk or deal with opposite sex.

More than girls, boys have pressure to perform better in life for good job with nice earning. Their marriageability usually depends on job and earning status. Even though young girls

---

Trust me I want to set you free.
I just don't know how.

Like you,
I never received any training,
To be a good husband or father,
I also have a child inside me.

Let us join hands,
Trust each other,
And create a better world.

---

prefer to spend time with smarter and stronger boys, they prefer to marry more economically settled boys. This indirectly puts huge pressure on boys. As they graduate, they gets sucked in job, marriage, fatherhood and child rearing challenges. By the time they realize, they are around 45-50 years old and wonder what the meaning of life is.

9.4   Importance of Exercise for Happiness

This book has amply highlighted the importance of flexibility exercise and swimming since childhood. This matter is expressed again to

Body is temple
Keep it Sacred
Keep it in shape

highlight the facts that it is now more important from the happiness and women's safety point of view. Both men and women in India rarely do exercise. As a result, they grow fat gradually with age and more so after marriage.

9.5   Exploitation as perceived from both side

Often we see a man, who has never hurt anyone before marriage, becomes a devil after marriage. He reacts to become abusive and violent and thus committing domestic violence. Sometime nagging wife is considered as a cause of this violence. Who is actually responsible for these problems?

Author does not claim to be an expert in this matter, but would like to share a few things, so that discussion can be triggered on similar lines. To the author, both the violent husband and the nagging wife are victims of the faulty education and distorted family upbringing problems. If we train the boys and girls a little bit about sexuality, moral issues, legal stands, sentiments and handling conflicting situations, things can be improved. Author would like to share a small real story here:

A family, married for three to four years, was undergoing stressful situation. The wife realised that she had conflicts and relationship problems with husband. She understood that she was nagging him regularly while he was becoming more abusive and violent.

She confided the problem to one of her uncles, whom she deeply respected. She was aware that even this uncle had also undergone similar problems in his life. She consulted him and asked, "Uncle! You have faced similar in later stage of married life, but why am I facing this problem so early? How it can be managed?"

Uncle asked about of her daily routine. The girl had her second child only six months back. Due to continuous baby crying, she was unable to sleep most nights. The child was usually wearing cloth napkin as advised by her family elders. Since a child takes milk every three hours, so it is normal to urinate in between. The discomfort of the wet cloth napkin woke up the child. So, the mother had to take care of the child almost every one and half hours interval and unable to sleep properly.

The uncle explained to her, that the baby feeding cycle cannot be changed. To match the baby sleep cycle, human body has a unique mechanism of deep and light sleep, with cycles of three hours. One may go back to sleep very fast if woken up in the light stage of sleep after every 3 hours. If one is woken in deep sleep period, getting back to sleep is difficult. Hence, if the mother sleeps with the child after the feeding, she will be able to wake up after three hours, feed the baby and go back to sleep easily. Now, when the mother again had to wake up to change the napkin, she cannot go back to sleep, creating fatigue and irritation.

So the first advice to her was very simple, "Use modern disposable napkin at least at night, this way the mother would be able to sleep better and provide quality time to family and husband"

Uncle further enquired, "Do you ever say – **TOUCH ME NOT**"*. The answer was positive from the girl. How the mother could be expected to participate in act of love when she had no physical energy. That means, there had been no sexual relationship for 9 months and additional 6 months by then.*

*So, the second advice from uncle was, "**Sleep well, feel strong and initiate regular sexual life for happiness**". But the girl was still sceptical as she was worried about her husband's physical abuse. The uncle then advised her to do an experiment to deal with husband abusive behaviour and violence. The experiment was*

When the husband is angry, first check if he is hungry. If yes, then feed him.

If no, catch his collar, pull him to bed and perform the act of love. Now that he is physically satisfied and he would never commit violence."

At this stage, she should enquire about the reason behind his anger. But the actual problem or the cause of anger must also be understood and taken care of. The act of love is in an instant medicine against violence like the role of paracetamol tablets against high fever.

The girl actually implemented this experiment and found it to be extremely effective. So the last advice is "Never use Touch me Not, it is worse than any form of physical violence. Men are weak. They are always scared about their capability. Men lose control when deprived. It is not easy for them.

*But this does not mean men have no responsibility. They have to be **kind and promise no physical violence at any cost**. When wife is nagging, anger is natural. **Recognize the trigger, and avoid conflict. Worst, get away.** Violence is not acceptable in any sense.*

This story is mentioned here, to inform participants to tell us more stories in similar lines such that this world becomes a better place to live for all of us.

9.6   Women and Education

Female child on an average outperforms their male counterpart in academic and many extra-curricular activities in India. The girl's better performance is reflected in the results of the 10th and 12th board examinations. On the other hand, boys perform better in sports and activities that require physical activities. However, female representation in engineering sector is very less in comparison to most sectors like medical, commerce and architecture.

This matter was discussed with Susanne, a handicap child care specialist. Her views were very touching and enlightening and the interaction is presented below without editing. She started her Master's degree in special child care after the birth of her first child in USA. Her experience as working and studying mother is shared below, in her own words. Here she had tried to highlight the fact that we need to make the education system which are friendly to women, where they are not forced to delay marriage just because they want to pursue higher education.

The academic and lifestyle adaptations by women:

A woman's' Perspective

Susanne is a bright professional woman from USA, married to an Indian engineer, at an age of 21 years. She had three issues. She worked in India for 6 years. However, she shifted to USA as she felt her children would do better under the educational system there. According to her, in USA, there is more stress sports and other activities. In studies, there is more emphasis on self-learning and projects. She generally visits India twice every year to offer professional services here.

The author raised the issue of less proportion of girls opting for engineering courses in India, "Susanne.

Do you think that girls in India are shying away from engineering sector since it requires longer period to establish oneself? Or, is it due to the social stereotyping that the girls have to focus on early marriage and having issues? The longer time to settle and also lack of child care support available to them, may be responsible for this scenario. Or, maybe it is due to the belief that they will get married, have babies and then not have time to dedicate to these further studies. But what about men? Don't they get married and often have children during these preparatory years? So is it the actual acts of marriage and births that prevent dedication? How you can compare it with the situation in USA?"

Susanne nodded and said thoughtfully, "You may be right. Juggling between career and family is a tough task, even in USA. In India, you have special problems of lack of family, societal and child care support. I can narrate you my tough experiences, which will lead you to analyze yourself how difficult it is or women to acquire professional degrees after child birth."

Susanne stopped for a while then resumed her sharing, "I will share with you my own post-graduate experience. I was in my first semester of my Master's degree and I was struggling desperately to juggle between my different roles- as a student, research assistant, wife and a mother of a 9 month old infant. I was so tired and frustrated that one day, I lamented to one of my professors that it was too much and I was considering dropping out. She stopped what she was doing and faced me with her full attention"

The professor said looking straight in her eyes, "Look, you're the best student in the class. Why should you adopt to everybody else's plans and schedules? You have important things to do with your time. Be efficient and make the others adapt to you and support you!"

The author asked, "I am really interested in knowing how you faced this difficult time. In India too, the career-women face severe problem and the lack of family and institutional support makes it tougher."

Susanne smiled and continued, "You are right. I was thinking of dropping my study, but these words changed the way I looked at things. Even in India, you can create support system, if you are willing. I stayed in the PG course and asked for support from every quarter. I took help from grannies, friends, family, and husband and managed my time in flexible way. I learnt how to ask and demand. My daughter was cared for by my best friends, my grandmother and occasional day-care provider. I remembered that my contribution was valuable and it was not me that was flawed but a system that forgot to include the family perspective."

This conversation forced the author into deep introspection. The contribution of women both the family and the society through their career is very important. When women participate equally with men, the female perspective would add to diversity and enrich any creative process. Women have legitimate right to purse their dream. This is pushing that average age of marriage and child birth. Can't we create a society where women can go for early marriage and child birth without compromising with their dream? To help women start life early, we need to provide strong support system and this can be analysed as follows:

a) **Good child care system:** In India, percentage of women perusing education after marriage is low compared to advanced countries. In fact, in India, most women give up work to take care of child birth and child care. This was also highlighted by Susanne. From this, it is clear that we need to implement Hoikuen and Shokudo concepts.

b) **Post Child-Birth Education and training:** It has been discussed that postponing marriage and motherhood is a recent phenomenon among educated families of India. So for a girl, she has two choice: postpone the marriage or expect to gain education after motherhood. Hence, the society should create an atmosphere where women can purse education and training even after marriage and childbirth.

9.7 Story of Women from across the World

Some countries are considered safe for women, while some countries are considered under turmoil and disturbed. All these countries have taken different routes to face the world of interaction and relationship between men and women. Japan, with a combination of Buddhist background and influence of modern society has created a very safe and non- discriminatory society. On the other hand, South America has created a liberal society that has lot of dance and music in life. The society in Russia and east European countries also deserve mention as they have been successful in sports. The artistic features of gymnastics on the floor shows that they have amalgamated sports and music in a big way. Russia has well developed universities that concentrate on science of sports, music and dance. Women have extracted rich dividend in sports arena and created equitable and happy society.

Hence, this project aims to collect and share life stories of women across different regions and cultures and see the world through their eyes. For the success of the project it is important that the women selected could express and articulate. Not everyone will be able to express themselves in an interesting way. Hence, proper care will be taken in selecting the participants, while minimising the chances of cultural bias and generalisation.

In the proposed series of study proper care will be taken in finalising the selection criteria. In first study, proposed here only one age group will be taken. Major selection criteria are:

- Age criteria.

- Cross culture spread by choosing them from distinct geographical location.

- Academic/ artistic background: Academically strong as well as successful ladies from artistic field (music, dance, movie, art, etc.) will be selected in equal ratio.

9.7.1 Age Criteria and its Justification

Women's life can be better compared if we select women of similar age in one study. It will lead to homogeneity in growth and experiences in same sample. Hence, the project will be carried out in stages for different age groups in series of study. With so many group- studies to be conducted, it will be an extensive project. Hence, in the initial stage, we propose to conduct cross cultural study of only group c). The groups planned for are:

a. 10-14 years: Representing the children growing up and facing their puberty.

b. 18-20 years: Representing the youth who have crossed their puberty. These children will share similar study, career selection process and sexual exposure

c. 28-32 years: Representing women who have finished their studies and are facing world. Some of them might have become married, while others are contemplating marriage.

d. 35-40 years: Representing women who has faced children growing up and all complex problems of the society. This group is possibly going through mid-life stage, where a void would come as their children are ready to leave home

e. 55-65 years : Representing the group that has seen the life and can tell us a lot

f. 70 years- plus: Representing the experienced and wisdom-souls.

9.7.2   Cross culture with distinct geographical location

India is obviously the first important choice. Dr. Gupta has lived in **Japan** for 12 years. He feels that he understands their culture well. The combination of Buddhist culture and modern society has created a free and fair but unique country. The Hoikuen concept presented in the book shows how much this country considers children as the most important asset for the country. Japan is also considered a country very safe for women. But, can this country be considered ideal? The third choice would be **west European countries** with unique history. Germany would be a good choice, but the selection would be open to other countries too. Russia would be the natural fourth choice for its contribution to sports. The fifth choice would **be Central or Southern African countries**. War torn and disturbed countries will be ignored. Only stable countries would be selected. The last group would be **South American countries** trying to get a glimpse of dance and music on life.

9.7.3   Academic background

This research will choose two groups of people. The first group will be chosen with **best of academic records**. This group will also be expected to create the documents and do the writing part. The other group will be selected from artistic field (music, dance, movie, art, etc.) to add colour to the project.

9.8   Expert Committee and Research

This group will be led by Dr. Supratic Gupta. Additional members will be selected from universities from across the world (may be from the proposed 5 regions) who will be able to extend these works to future research through doctoral studies for their students.

As new conclusion and results comes out, there will in a necessity to carry out scientific survey to understand if they represent the average trend or not.

I CAN BE THE FIRE
I CAN BE THE QUEEN
I CAN BE THE BALLERINA
STANDING ON MY TOES
I CAN BE THE WARMTH
I CAN BE THE WISDOM
BUT, I AM NOT A LABEL
DESIGNED BY YOU

- Divya Singh

9.9 Methodology

Dr. Gupta will be controlling the pace of the first project with the support of the committee. The work will be undertaken by Supratic Trust for Research and Incubation (STRI). Candidates would be invited to apply from across the world. English knowledge is necessary. Expert committee of professors from across the world capable of guiding students for doctoral degree in similar lines will also be invited. This can become a part of research portal development too.

To share the life experience is not easy. One may write or express themselves by expressing themselves through video/ audio recording which will be easily possible through their mobile. Group session or question answers will be planned as necessary. This project is expected to be completed within 3 months period of interaction and payment is expected to be paid to the participants and the committee members. The methodology undertaken is:

- Women in cross cultural setting have different and unique experiences regarding their growing up, sexuality, career and relationship.

- We want to understand their life experiences in their own words, written preferably or in video and audio format

- The research study across 4 continents and 5 countries including India, will help in making a comparative study in the 5-8 parameters, which will be defined in the beginning.

- The study will be published in the book format, so that the whole world is made aware of the challenges and the important issues concerning the post-modern women in 21st century.

- The study will help us to evolve more awareness on these issues.

9.10   Proposed Programme Activities

We will select and Shortlist 10 women Volunteers; 2 each from regions of the world as given in the section 4.0. The volunteers selected will be willing to share about their life experiences in voice recording or written format, and submit it to the research coordinator. It will be later developed by a team of content writers in a comparative research book format.

The women volunteers' selection criteria, will be decided on the basis of their education, career and age group. Half of the volunteers will be from academic and carrier oriented women and the other half will be from performing arts. After selection, all these 10 women will be oriented by the Research Coordinator regarding the parameters on which they will share their experiences in audio or video recordings. The Parameters of sharing the life experiences will be broadly covering incidents, events and feeling associated with following:

- Childhood (Friends, Parents, Games, First School)

- Adolescence (Study, Friends, Parents, Sexuality, Sexual experiences)

- Youth (Career Choice, Colleges, Relationship, Sexuality)

- Early Adult hood (Marriage, Job and Child Birth)

The comparative study will be made on the above criteria. The Volunteers will be sharing their life stories with in a period of 2 months. Their privacy will be protected and those who want their anonymity; will be granted it. They will be paid allowances for participation and transferring the copyrights to the STRI (Supratic Trust of Research and Incubation) who can publish the study too, being the implementing agency.

Sharing will be done on audio recording, video recording, Skype or voice chat. The research coordinator may ask additional question and clarification from the volunteers if it is needed.

The research work will be shared with the policy makers, media and leading institutions and advocate or formulate programmes for empowering the women in family, society and work place. The study will also help in comparative studies of the impact made by the cultural and social values and attitudes, regarding the feminism and women empowerment issues.

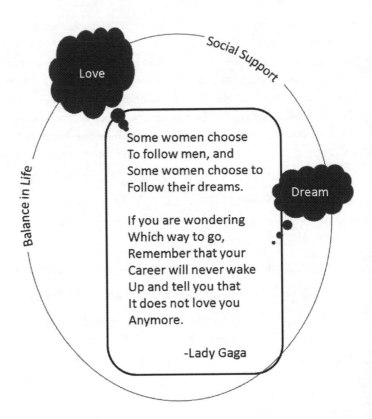

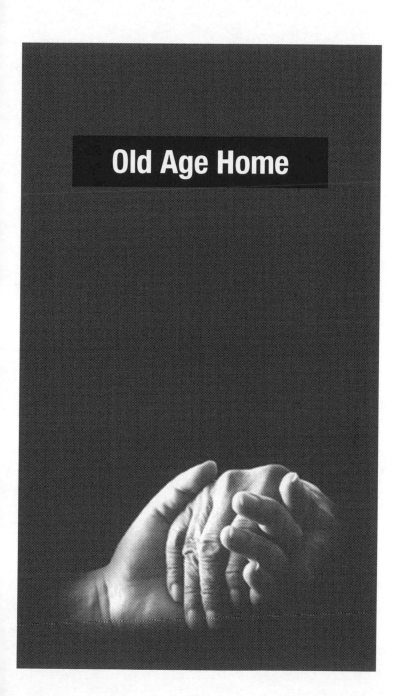

Old Age Home

CHAPTER 10
OLD AGE HOME

10.1 Introduction

Old age is a natural cycle of human growth, which is often not understood in its real sense in Indian society. Indian society, on one hand, gives much reverence and respect to the age in theoretical and cultural context; while on the

> We often tend to forget that
> Each old person has a child
> Struggling within.
> S/he also want to
> Dance, sing and enjoy life.
>
> They also wish to share
> The responsibility of life.

other hand, we often seen gross neglect and apathy for the older people, getting more prevalent among the families in the cities and the villages. We tend to forget that each old person has a child struggling with in him; the child which has existed inside life long, but which has manifested fully in the old age. That child in the old person needs not only food and shelter but also love, care, friendship, companionship and trust. People like to enjoy life, laugh and sing. This does not change as we grow old. Often we become useless for the society. We have to fit into the role model expected from us.

Author Dr. Supratic Gupta, faculty IIT Delhi has observed the plight of the senior citizens closely. Two years back, he had befriended a retired man

> **You are never too old to set another goal or to dream a new dream.**
>
> **C. S. Lewis**

of 72 years, whom he met quite accidently in a park. Their friendship blossomed much and they started going to movies and malls together sometimes and enjoyed everything like excited children. But what surprised him was the reaction of the old man from a well-off family. They mentally resented the author for visiting the old man and offering him time, psychological support and fun. Perhaps, the family was feeling guilty and jealous both, since they were giving the basic facilities but not the much needed gestures of love, which makes an old person happy. Old men feel more neglected sometimes, since their spouse gets busy in grandchildren and making attempt to maintain cordial relationship with the daughter-in-laws and sons.

The author wants to find a way so that this gap in the needs and requirements in the old age is fulfilled, through a model old age care home, where all sections of people are benefitted. The proposed old age home will not only take care of the old persons, who can afford it, but also some needy poor men & women, whose expenses are, sponsored though contributions, donations, grants and sponsorship.

10.2   Current Status of Old Age Care Centres

Old age homes are meant for senior citizens who are unable to stay with their families or are destitute. Only some states in India such as Delhi, Kerala, Maharashtra and West Bengal have developed good quality old age homes. These old age homes have special medical facilities for senior citizens such as mobile health care systems, ambulances, nurses and provision of well-balanced meals. But conditions prevailing in 90% of the old age homes are dismal. There are more than a thousand old age homes in India, including the government run centres. Only some of them offer free accommodation. Some homes work on a payment basis depending on the type and quality of services offered.

Indian society on one hand, give much reverence and respect to the aged in theoretical and cultural context.

But their right to enjoy life in often curbed, as they have to be a lead role model for the grand-children growing up.

The concept of the old age home has become quite familiar today, but often for the wrong reasons. The idea seems to evoke a sigh of pity which is uncalled for. Firstly, it has been ascertained by social surveys that there need not be any stigma attached to the residents of old age homes and neither do they require our pity. Secondly, many parents of middle class families are neither neglected nor abandoned by their children. But, in this age of MNCs and FDIs, working professionals today are compelled to move away from home and work in faraway places. The elders of such families often do not wish to live permanently with their children in strange and distant places. Except for visits, they prefer to be live in their own homes. We have to create a place, where this feeling of alienation is neutralised by an atmosphere of companionship and bonding between the old persons.

Apart from food, shelter and medical amenities, some old age homes also provide other entertainment activities to senior citizens. Some old age homes have day care centres. These centres only take care of senior citizens during the day. Lack of transparency and poor standard of services are visible in most

of the homes. There is also lack of emotional and psychological support in most of the current old age homes. We want to change these conditions through a model old age home, in which all type of supports are provided.

10.3 Objectives & Facilities

The objectives of the proposed old age home is to create a place where the physical, medical, psychological, social and emotional needs of the old persons are satisfied in a justifiable manners. This old age home will be primarily for the well settled persons, who can afford to invest and pay its expenses in a planned manner. But at least 25% of the seats will be kept for the needy and poor men and women, whose expenses will be met from contributions and sponsorship - corporate as well as individual. In this way, both sections of society will get a chance to foster emotional bonds and companionship, to create a happy place. This ideal home will have lot of scope for entertainment quotients- the songs, movies, dance, bhajans and clubs; so that the child inside each old person is nurtured. Apart from nutritional foods and hygienic residence, full-fledged medical facilities will be provided. Proper care will be taken to provide companionship and comradeships among the inmates of the homes. The following facilities are expected in the old age home:

- We will create a safe and happy haven, with a family like atmosphere among the residents. Senior citizens will experience a sense of security and friendship, when they share their joys and sorrows with each other.

- All basic facilities like hygienic rooms, toilets, kitchens, common rooms, nutritional food and security will be provided. There will be team professional people from hospitality industry to manage the things

- All type of medical facilities will be provided. There will be tie-ups with doctors, hospitals and medical facilities. There will be a full time trained nurse, residing inside the home.

- Psychological, social support and counselling services will be available on regular basis under a team of professional social workers, medical personnel and psychologists.

- There will be 2 types of payments systems for the inmates. 75% of the residents will be paying for all the services provided. It will be including admission charges, annual and monthly payment. Rest of the 25% of inmates, who will be mostly from poor sections of society, will be just paying a nominal monthly fee. Their expenses will be covered from sponsorship and donations.

- There will be also a provision of advance booking of a place in the home, 5 years before; on annual instalments payment systems. It will make the home finance sustainable.

- The old age home will encourage bonding, Jodi and even long relationship between the inmates. At this age they need a partner more. We will explore the legal issue of companionship and live-in relationship among the inmates. It will be purely consensual partnership. It will make them happy. There may be JODI or Buddy system also, breaking the barrier of caste and class. Even the poor person can bond with rich person. It depends upon their compatibility.

- There will lot of entertainment activities -- the songs, movies, dance, bhajans and outings; so that the child inside each old person is nurtured. It will create a happy place.

- Nuclear families may leave their children here to experience of companionship of older generations as grandparents. It will also provide much needed breathing space and time for young couples who rarely get time for each other while taking care of the child.

The author has observed the pangs of the loneliness of old people, who are not taken care of by their children. He wants to build an ideal home, with strong personal bonds. He wants to create a place, where he can also live in old age; a place, where all can live with dignity, respect, love, entertainment and companionship.

10.4   Social Responsibility Factor
This old age home will also satisfy duties to the society wherever possible. There are many families where children do not get the love of grandparents. To a child, it is the love and the age that matters:

- Couples without grandparents in same city can have associated relationship with the elders residing in old age home.

- It can also serve as an occasional childcare centre when young father and mother can leave the child.

- The people here will have lot of time. They can undertake lot of social service activities, from pre and post-birth care, counselling, etc.

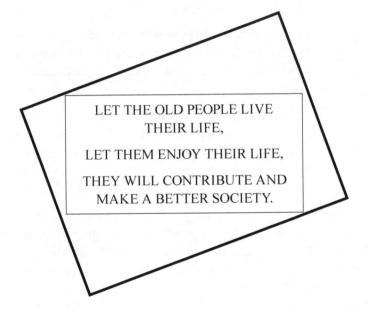

LET THE OLD PEOPLE LIVE THEIR LIFE,

LET THEM ENJOY THEIR LIFE,

THEY WILL CONTRIBUTE AND MAKE A BETTER SOCIETY.

Scientific
Thinking

CHAPTER 11
SCIENTIFIC THINKING

11.1   Introduction

Thinking is perhaps the most important human evolutionary function. In fact, we survive, grow and thrive by thinking process. Human thinking is the highest stage of evolution of

The objective of this document is to fill this gap by explaining the scientific way of thinking and its applicability in life.

consciousness, which sets it apart from the animal species. Most of the inventions in past have occurred due to our ability to think about various phenomena or natural events or problems. Newton's curiosity to know the reason behind the falling apple led to the invention of gravitational theories. There are numerous similar examples, which have led homo sapiens to evolve into a highly developed industrialized civilization. The statement "I think, therefore I am" by the French philosopher Rene Descartes shows the importance of thinking.

It is a known fact that thinking is inherently related to the processes of being aware and gaining knowledge. These processes, in turn, depend on certain subjects and methods which have come to be collectively known as science. The definition of science has widened in the last 3-4 centuries. It is clear that it is a tool in the hands of a curious and inquiring mind to understand natural phenomena using logic, reasoning

First, have a definite, clear practical ideal; a goal, and objective. Second, have the necessary means to achieve your ends; wisdom, money, materials, and methods. Third, adjust all your means to that end.

-Aristotle

and verifiable experiments. It is a way of knowing. The fact of the matter is that science has helped humankind to progress a lot thorough development of understanding and knowledge of a variety of natural and social phenomena. Is science the study of the natural and the physical world? Or, is it about the specialized knowledge of any subject? Or, is it one of the many acceptable ways of knowing and understanding various personal, natural and social phenomena? It appears that the efforts towards finding one correct answer are of not much use. What is more important here is to understand what science, like other subjects, does for the individuals and the society? Another good explanation suggested by Moore is that *science is a human endeavour - done by human beings to answer questions of human interest or human importance.*

All of us think on various personal and social aspects of our lives. Some issues demand deeper thinking while others do not. While doing all this, we hardly "think" about the "thinking process" itself or raise question like – is there a scientific way of thinking?

When people think or do something, they just do it instinctively. It has also been noticed that even students at IITs are unable to write the documents objectively. The reason is that they learn how to solve problems, but they cannot write because they have not been taught how to write. Most often people interact with each other, they talk without bothering about the objective or draw conclusion after the talk or work for better output in future. To overcome this, the author wishes to extend the basic method of research to all other aspects of life. A research student is usually asked to follow a set pattern of thinking trying to understand the objective, know what others have done in similar lines, and draw proper conclusions. The objective of this chapter is to present this method as the scientific way of thinking and explain its applicability in life. While presenting

Science	Religion
Hypothesis	*Religion and Most Life Activity*
Experiment & Verification	*Depend on Feeling*
Observation Repeatability & Conclusion	*And* *Not Science*
Scientific Thinking	
Objective	Applicable to
Literature Review	a) Research Activity
Content & Action	b) Any Real Life
Conclusion	c) Religious Action

any event or taking action in life, most people forget their objective. Through this process, most people would be able to take life more easily and explain their thought to others in a structured manner.

11.2   Discussion and Analysis

Scientific thinking is a way of thinking that should help us in all stages of life. Scientific thinking, as per author's definition, is a simple yet effective way of thinking about anything in life. Any issue or problem or phenomenon has to be approached with a structured thinking consisting of four parts, which are: **(1) Objective, (2) Literature Review, (3) Content and (4) Conclusion.**

The first two parts are extremely important as they provide the basis of the starting point for any activity. Most researchers start work without understanding the objective of their work. They keep on performing experiments, often to find that they have overdone their experiments or deviated from the objectives. Objective must be defined in each and every activity of our life. It can dynamically change as we gain experience.

To explain the importance of having a clear objective in all aspects of life, let us take the example of the curriculum in school in India. From the childhood, we are instructed to read and memorize books and are required to reproduce what we have learned in the exams. We never ever bother to question honestly, why we are studying a particular subject. Let us take the topic of study of biology. Most children find it boring. If we explain to the children that studying biology is important as the child would understand his/her body, know what and how to eat, how this would affect his/her growth, strength and energy, then the student will find the subject more interesting. For the subject of history, a child from north east often finds lack of interest as he wonder why he has to study the history of North India, where none of his own regional history is taught. Even if we look at mathematics it is not the favorite subjects of a majority of students for similar reasons. One of the plausible explanations of this is that most of us do not understand or appreciate the objective behind studying mathematics and our interest or inclination is lost in mathematical theories and equations. Similar logic can be applied to all subjects. Hence, it is important that we define objective of each activity to be more effective.

Hence, the objective of studying a subject should be explained to the student in a way that the reader can appreciate the subject and take interest. Often we underestimate what a child is able to understand. If this system is followed, then there will be more and more "learners" and "practitioners" of a subject than mere students. Students will do self-study and learn more to satisfy his objective.

The author emphasizes that if the objective of any work is well defined, backed by references, the purpose of learning would become more interesting and meaningful. We would then understand each and every aspect of our life. It would become more meaningful if we understand the objective of our work, if we have sufficient capability to do the work, or if it is worthy to do the work. All our action might be totally different from what we are doing today. It might make us think that our life would become more mechanical. However, this is not true. On the contrary, our life would become more meaningful and beautiful. Life is mechanical when we live without thinking about the objectives behind our actions.

Literature review, the second part, is the investigation process, where a researcher looks at past about what work has been done in relevant fields, the approaches, results, ways of thinking, etc. Usually, in a scientific research, the researcher goes through published journals, conference proceedings, theses, and now-a-days even from web sites. This is a very important step that makes clear to the reader, the state-of-art in the relevant field and the gaps in knowledge.

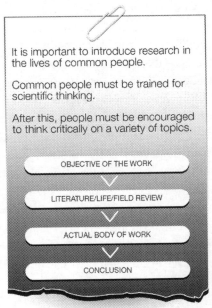

It is important to introduce research in the lives of common people.

Common people must be trained for scientific thinking.

After this, people must be encouraged to think critically on a variety of topics.

OBJECTIVE OF THE WORK

LITERATURE/LIFE/FIELD REVIEW

ACTUAL BODY OF WORK

CONCLUSION

In life, we may or may not be able to always read scientific journals for reference. While a girl is pregnant, it would be wise if she reads some books on pregnancy and its other aspects. She may get the required information from elders also. Either way it helps.

The third part, the content of the research is the main body part of the research, where the hypotheses and the basic assumptions are tasted, based on the actual data from the field. It is the actual work itself. Finally, the importance of the conclusion after the actual activity cannot be undermined.

11.3   Life Examples
It would be worthwhile to take a look at the following life examples to appreciate the concept of the author.

a.   Suppose a boy wants to propose a girl. How he should go about it through the method of scientific thinking. First, he should define truthfully to himself what he wants (Objective). Does he want a life partner or girlfriend for a short time or just a friend? Secondly, he should know how similar problem has been addressed by people in similar or dissimilar situation, the possible outcome and how to handle different types of situations (Literature Review). Now, if he does this, after having a clear objective and realizing the consequence of his action based on information from past cases, his chances of success will be increased. After the act, it is also important to introspect and check and conclude if the objectives have been satisfied or not.

b.   A school girl came to an engineering college professor to understand maths and physics. The teacher explained the concepts with a bird's eye view of the subject. This helped the girl understand the concepts. The teacher explained to her that any student would understand a subject easier if she looks at the subject with a bird's eye view and do some self-study. With time, the girl started coming to the professor again and again to study with him. Though this helped her, the professor asked her to refrain from this as she is not building her inner strength in this process. Over-dependence is not good. This way, the professor explained to the girl that one must have clear objective in mind. One should ask help, only when s/he has tried and failed to understand the concepts. One must try and build his/her inner strength.

c. When a Ph.D. student or a researcher wants to select a guide and choose a topic of research, he should think of his future and decide the broad topic of interest. Then, he should look for a guide who has worked in similar lines and acquaint himself of the publications of the guide in that field. This will help him when he interacts with the guide. He must be flexible and willing to learn as per guide's instruction. Clarity of mind would help him select guide and fix a research topic appropriately.

1.2   Conclusion

The author has attempted to explain the concept of scientific thinking and its practical, day-to-day applications. This is a simple but powerful technique with many benefits. One must practice the same before gaining mastery over it. Once you have understood the concept and its application, the benefits may be experienced in the form of higher success rate. The author has decided to make short movies in future to high light the importance and significance of scientific thinking process with the 4 steps clearly highlighted.

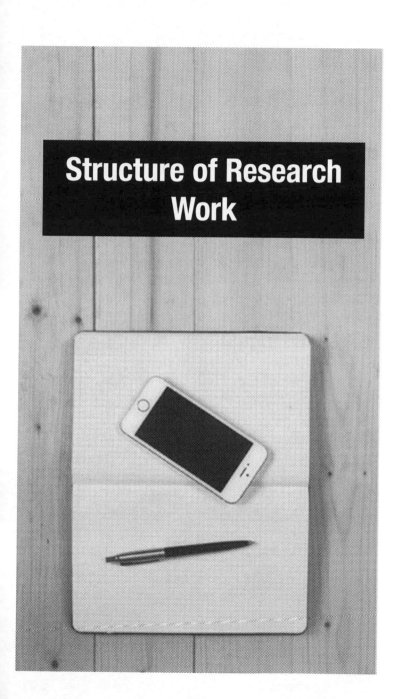

Structure of Research Work

CHAPTER 12
STRUCTURE OF RESEARCH WORK

12.1   Introduction

In India, the learning efforts of a university student end with a Ph.D. He/she then pursues either an academic or a corporate career depending on personal choice or other factors. The process of earning a Ph.D. is quite tough and one has to be very methodical in conducting doctoral research and then reporting the findings in the form of a thesis. In pursing high level of research, it is important to understand the structure of a thesis. This document is presented so that readers can also follow similar format while writing any document.

12.2   Structure of a Thesis

Author feels that it is important to understand how a how a typical doctoral thesis looks like. The thesis usually has a cover page, acknowledgement, abstract, and table of content, list of tables, figures and symbols.

In the **Acknowledgement** section, one has to give formal thanks to the guide/s and the other people who have assisted in completing the research. This is followed by acknowledging the sponsoring agency, if any available. The rest of section depends on the student. Often family members and friends are also acknowledged. Some people also thank God. This is a personal chapter.

The **Abstract** is a short summary of the complete book, explaining the need for the research, method adopted, major conclusions and contributions of the research work, such that reader may understand content of the thesis.

This is followed by **actual chapters** and **reference list**. One must note that each and every chapter in itself will have an introduction, clearly defining the objective of the chapter and finally having a conclusion.

Chapter 1 is usually called **Introduction**. It

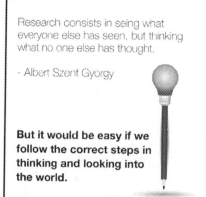

Research consists in seing what everyone else has seen, but thinking what no one else has thought.

- Albert Szent Gyorgy

But it would be easy if we follow the correct steps in thinking and looking into the world.

obviously defines the objective of the work. It starts with a story explaining the topic leading to how the objective of the work is important, going through a small series of literature review to highlight the importance. Finally, in this chapter, the content of the thesis is explained. This chapter also defines the basic assumptions, limitations and the method of research adopted.

The second chapter is usually a **Literature Review.** A literature review is never a collection of short review of various works. It is actually a monologue of the author trying to highlight the importance of the work, state-of-the-art in such a way that he explains the approach taken in the thesis. He speaks subject wise on the way referring to various people's research to highlight the matter. If one reads this literature review, it is obvious that author wants to study a topic where lot of work has been done, but still there is much scope of new work which could be done.

Except in the chapter on "Hoikuen" and "Music and Dance for Street Children", Literature Review is not presented in other chapters of this book. So, authors accepts that this book should not be considered as a scientific document. The authors could have spent a little more time to research on each of these chapters.

The objective of this book is to present the innovative and wild thoughts of Dr. Gupta. It is presented with a hope that these concepts will be discussed and researched further by public/private/government agencies, which take appropriate steps to ask researchers to do research and implementation of these concepts.

Usually the third chapter is more **theoretical**. It builds the theory utilized in this research based on past work and explains the methodology of experiments/analytical research/survey work to be adapted in the work. The parameters used in this research are clearly defined in this chapter.

After the third chapter, we have a series of chapters which elaborate the work done in a logical way. As explained before, each chapter also starts with an introduction, its short objective, methodology adopted, work done and conclusion.

One might feel that there is duplication in the literature review and objective writing but this is necessary as in first and second chapter, objectives and literature review were written from a global point of view. The theory chapter had already given the details. So, in these chapters a short recapitulation is important. Obviously, each chapter must end with conclusion.

The last chapter is usually the **conclusion** chapter. This chapter starts with the small story with which we started in the introduction chapter. A short review of the objective and methodology is explained. Finally, we write the conclusion and future recommendations. This is usually done by compiling the conclusion of all the previous chapters in a logical flow.

These instructions are the personal views of Dr. Supratic Gupta and may not represent the writing style of thesis of other researchers. Dr. Gupta himself wrote his thesis on these guidelines and has guided students to follow them.

12.3 Graphical and Pictorial Presentation

Graphical or pictorial presentation is a very important part of a scientific document. The thought process has to be divided parameter wise. The effect of each parameter is represented graphically. Often equations and dependences are quantified either based on mathematical formulation or experimental results. These are always based on some simplifying assumption. Life is always more complex, yet in a research one has to define assumptions and limitations.

It is important to present good pictures, diagrams and charts that represent the thoughts of the author as they often express much more compared to the words. In children book, often a page is filled with colourful pictures and have a few words.

12.4 Slide Preparation

Creating a strong presentation is very important. It must be remembered that pictorial representations speaks better than words. One must understand the audience before making the presentation. It should start with one-two slide with the story or back ground leading to the objective. The assumptions and limitations should be explained. The method or theory adopted should be explained in short emphasising the critical points. Finally, the most important data should be presented followed by the conclusions.

The time slot allocated for the presentation should be kept in mind. The listener's concentration span should be consider while making presentation. One should attempt using animation to make better presentation. Trial practice or rehearsal is very important.

12.5   Practice and Presentation

The final part of any research is presentation. One must practice many times to see how the presentation feels like. One may practice presentation in front of his guide or some friends to get proper feedback. It should not fall short or cross the time allocated with big margin. During the presentation, eye contact with audience is very important. It is important to undertake strategic pause, to make sure the audience following or not. If the topic is difficult, one may have to give simplifying explanations.

12.6   Facing Question and Answer Session

This part is often the most important part. For a good presentation, it is very important to have clear knowledge of the topic in hand. However, the listener would listen the presentation from his own knowledge and view point. He may ask a question that is beyond the scope of the topic or the knowledge of presenter. In such case, it is not recommended that the presenter attempt to answer the question by hook or crook. Answer like the following are good ways to tackle the questions:

- "This matter asked is beyond the scope of presentation",

- "Your question is good, but I am unable to answer you now and will get back to you later", etc.

Research Portal

CHAPTER 13
RESEARCH PORTAL

13.1 Introduction

The status of research culture in our country is still in nascent stage. This is more particularly true for the realms of research on the social-economic and developmental issues, which are of much importance for the general masses. When we talk about research, we generally connote it with the government funded research in the Institutes, or the Industry funded projects for their specific needs of production, sales and marketing. Government is the major funding organization for the research projects, whereas the industry funds in much lower proportion.

We rarely think of public funding and public participation in research in a systematic way. In the current scenario, the research studies are mostly done for publications, credits and promotion. Researchers are only concerned about what is publishable and what gives them academic achievement and promotion. This is creating a big problem as most of the research are rarely relevant to the needs and aspiration of the society or contribute positively to the national development. This includes research done in IITs or any universities, where students get masters or doctoral degrees.

Currently, most of the research fund is provided to engineering, manufacturing and medical/pharmaceutical fields. The investment in research related to social problems and issues are proportionately less. The overall picture of research in India is very poor, quantitatively as well as qualitatively. To maintain a healthy momentum of growth, the nation needs to invest at least 2 per cent of its GDP in R&D, as opposed to the 0.6 per cent currently allocated to it. If we look at the

Global Innovation Index in 2009, India is ranked 62. While at the Global Competitive Index, it is placed at 56. Government funding is not expected to increase, drastically in current decade. Though companies can invest part of its CSR budget in research, this is also not happening in big way. Our concern is that the general public is not aware of the different social and technical researches being carried out by educational and research institutes.

There is also lack of awareness and participation in research among the general public. Since public funding has its own restraints and limiting factors, we have to look at the other options of mobilizing funds through private initiatives, public participation though individual/institutional support and web-based *Crowd Funding*.

The author in this chapter proposes a unique concept to increase transparency through developing a research portal. The aim is to promote a culture in such a way that public will be able to know what research is going in various research institutes across the country. The researcher would share their work on the portal as well as pitch for their sponsorship and rating of their proposed research project.

In addition, general public and intellectuals can float/propose topics on the portals which will be opened to voting, rating and sponsorship. The public will bid for fund and/or votes that would create rating based on which the pulse of the public demand will be understood, analysed and rated. The CSR and Government would be motivated to fund and sponsor these researches in this public demand driven portal system. The author wants to give emphasis on research related to social sector that effect different aspects of life, like safety of women, education, changes required in the society, etc.

13.2 Concept

The basic objective of this research portal is to promote and support transparency and public participation in research at national level, which is the need of present society. The present research culture needs drastic changes. Author proposes the establishment of the following model for creating an all-inclusive model of research portal;

a) Creation of a public demand driven portal, which serves as common web-based platform of researchers, public, institutes and private/ public agencies and organizations

b) One of its mandate will be to let the researcher publish their proposals as well as to pitch in for sponsorship/ funds/ rating for their proposed new researches

c) The general public and intellectuals would be able to select and float new topics on the portal, more relevant with their needs and requirement and which will be opened to voting, rating and sponsorship by all, as per a system of responses on the portal. The responses will range from clicking support, votes comments, liking and sponsoring.

d) A Rating system will be created for each proposed topics for research, which will be based upon the number of votes and the monetary support pledged for the topics.

e) There will be 2 type of rating system; one which will rate the research topics, which have to be funded from the domain resources generated at the portal and the other rating will be of the researcher's quality and performance. The rating will be open to all stakeholders in some pre-defined categories.

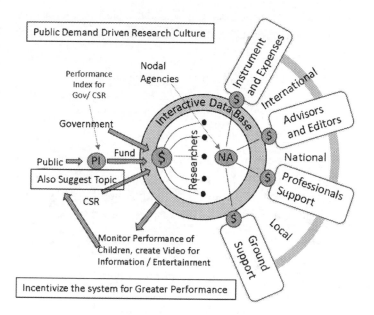

f) Private company and government can use these indexes of ratings to provide financial support topic wise or to promising individual researchers.

g) There will be online payment links for getting the research papers and also for sponsoring a particular research.

h) All the journals and research papers will be the copy righted and in later stage the control of research agenda and resources must be handed over to general public.

i) This online Portal may be later dedicated to the Nation, where all research Papers & journals are up loaded, shared, and disseminated.

13.3 Outcomes

The creation of the research portal will create a much conducive atmosphere for public-demand driven researches, on the topics which are more relevant to our social, economic and technological problems. It will lead to a significant positive change in our research culture. The following outcomes are expected:

a) General public will be linked with the ongoing researches, being made aware of relevant research being carried out in our country. This will bring about participatory research culture in our country.

b) The Public participation and ownership inherent in this concept will create more accountability for the researcher and research institutes. Currently, there is very poor accountability system in our research institutions.

c) Research will be initiated by public demand and necessity. It will cover all the social research topics for cultivating a public-oriented research culture, where the needs and aspirations of the masses is shared, disseminated and given shapes of grass root plans. It will create a demand as well meet this demand by creating more research

d) The portal will also enable and empower a common person to raise his or her voice for conducting research in areas where the society desperately needs introspection and research.

e) The portal will be based on a sustainable business model, where funds from public, private and Government will be effectively be used.

f) The collective power of such voices will eventually force the government to allocate and utilize research infrastructure and resources as per the demands of the people.

The portal is conceptualized to rectify the huge gaps between demand and supply so far as research is concerned. There is very less industry sponsored research that take place in Indian universities and technical institutions. What is required by the society is not done by the researchers; and what the researcher does is not required by the society. This is leading to an imbalance of dangerous proportion which, if not corrected in time, may result into permanent collapse of the research system in our country. This public driven system hopefully will make the research be more relevant.

Research Environment in India

CHAPTER 14
RESEARCH ENVIRONMENT IN INDIA

14.1   Introduction

Any modern society would require sincere research, analysis and introspection in all human and scientific fields to grow and excel. In scientific terminology, the term research has specific meaning and connotations. A typical researcher identifies the problems, its objectives and tries to analyse and address the problem from a newer perspective, with an aim of creating a better world. Most of the research works are supported by government funds and partially some of them are initiated by industry sponsored projects.

The researcher has to publish his findings in research journals, which goes through rigorous steps of evaluation, before being published. It is expected that industry and the other stakeholders would pick up results and the outcomes of the researched knowledge to create a better world. We have to look up the research and its importance vis-à-vis its prevalence in developing and the developed world. There is much disparity between the nature, quality and funding of the research in different parts of the world. The modern civilisation is too much dependent upon the research to sustain and maintain its developmental momentum and sustainability of newer technologies.

What is the research but a blind date with knowledge?

-    *Will Harvey*

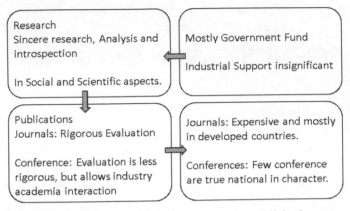

Research
Sincere research, Analysis and introspection

In Social and Scientific aspects.

Mostly Government Fund

Industrial Support insignificant

Publications
Journals: Rigorous Evaluation

Conference: Evaluation is less rigorous, but allows industry academia interaction

Journals: Expensive and mostly in developed countries.

Conferences: Few conference are true national in character.

Developed countries have their own well established systems of reputed journals, being published in all subjects, fields and professional areas. But in India, there is dearth of good quality and internationally accepted journals. Researchers in most developing countries like India prefer to publish their research work in international journals located in developed countries. These journals are expensive for the industry too. These publications are mostly for evaluation of the researchers for their promotion purpose, rather than for the betterment of society that provides financial grants to support the research.

14.2 National Conferences

In parallel to the researches being published on journals, all countries have their system of national conferences. This is much cheaper and more effective medium of communication and interface between the researchers and industry. The author is from Civil Engineering Department and hence has provided illustration and example of his department; but most of the points would be more or less applicable to all disciplines. He also provides examples from Japan and USA to prove his point.

In India, the national and international conferences are of trivial matter, in most cases and done just for the sake of formality. The quality of the papers presented in these conferences is mostly of sub- standard without providing any benefit to the Industry. Some time, it happens that one of the IITs, IISC Bangalore, NITs or some reputed research body, will initiate a conference and people who are friendly to it would participate. Industry would be least interested in it and often do not participate enthusiastically.

> *Proposal for National Conference*
>
> *Only one conference in each subject/sub-subject.*
>
> *Rotated across the country.*
>
> *Each City would have some conference to host.*
>
> *Big economic even and service industry would get boast.*
>
> *Will enhance industry-academia interaction.*
>
> *Participation and generated from industry and public should be encouraged.*
>
> *As people would travel across the country, it will contribute towards national integration.*

In this Chapter, the author presents briefly the research scenario in Japan and USA and makes the case of promoting more industry friendly national conferences in India, in all relevant subjects and themes.

14.3 Research Environment in Japan and USA

In Japan and USA, there is well established and reputed societies- Japanese Society of Civil Engineers (JSCE) and American Society of Civil Engineers (ASCE) respectively. These organizations also get government grants but mostly sustain themselves by the earning from membership and selling the journals. These organizations have their journals and hold periodic national and international conferences. Most of the students join the organization as a student and continue to be its member rest of the life. The private companies are also member to these organizations. As a result, these organization has a huge earning.

RESEARCH ENVIRONMENT IN INDIA

The author specializes in material research of concrete as a construction material. In Japan, concrete industry is also well stabilised and resourceful and has their independent group called Japan Concrete Institute (JCI).

Both JCI and JSCE hold regular conferences that are attended by all students and faculty of the country. Since all faculties and students attend it, most civil engineering companies also put demonstration booths and sponsor these conferences. These conferences become the most important event in that subject, where faculty and students present their work and take feedback from the industry. The industry can also select bright students for employment from these conferences. On the other hand, the industry also share their experiences and problems in these conferences and initiate the industry-academia interaction. Japan is one of the rare countries in the world, where engineers get higher respect than the management professionals. As a result, more students continue to Masters Level of these engineering courses before joining the industry.

These organizations are financially sound. They also receive governmental support but they are mostly self – reliant. These organizations also provide funds for research. They make research groups in such a way that the subjects relevant to the country are addressed properly.

These conferences are attended by large number of people. Hence, it becomes major financial activity in the city, where it is held. The hospitality industry with hotel rooms are mostly utilized. Mostly these conferences are organized in such way that each student doing their undergraduate or master thesis can present their findings. In Japan, the academic session end on 31st March. So the publications have to be submitted in March and the conferences are usually held in summer vacation time. Thus, the students doing doctoral studies and independent research can also present their work. The work from research institutes are more rigorously checked, while papers from industry are leniently allowed so that the interaction increases.

These conferences become big economic events for the cities. These conferences are rotated all across the country. Since there is a large number of subjects, each city invariably get its share of organizing the conferences every year in a sustainable manner. In India, most conferences are not national in character. There is no systematic plan in organising it. Its participants list is limited and mostly they are organized by a group of researchers. The number of conferences organized also count in the promotion and hence the participation is never planned national in character. This is true in most subjects except a few cases.

Indian Government should make it a priority, that industry-academia interaction is increased in numbers. In the beginning, the faculty members have to be forced to accept and made to participate these national conference. Gradually this culture of national conference will become an integral part of research calendar. This should be encouraged in all subjects, and not just engineering and medical fields. The conferences should be rotated across the country each year. The Indian government should also make efforts to promote and support establishment of journals in all subjects. They should support it financially in first stage and later these journals would develop into sustainable revenue generating. It will help much in the inducting research culture in India and benefitting the society in a big way. The government can establish similar integrated Journal system to benefit the development in our society.

14.4 Honorarium to Faculty in Projects

In India, research is mostly sponsored by the Government. It is a wishful thinking that industry or society should sponsor more of the research. Till that happens, it is worthy to analyse the funding situation in India.

It may be an exaggeration, but researchers conduct research mostly to satisfy their academic promotion requirements. Hence, most of the time it is witnessed that it is only the young researchers that apply for the research grant. This is mainly because Indian Government does not give honorarium for research work. Government feels that it pays salary, and hence they should not ask for honorarium. But without incentive, the system does not work and is not realistic. It is often seen that senior professors loose interest in research as there is nothing more to achieve. Non-provision of honorarium also encourages the possibility of false bills and degradation of research atmosphere.

It is proposed that honorarium be provided to researcher, as a parentage of the project fund. This percentage should be low for projects that have large expenses. On the other hand, this honorarium can be as high as 100% for projects with fewer expenses.

This will surely increase the number of applications for research funding. If National conference system is established, that can also be a way of evaluation. With time, the amount of funding from industry and society is expected to increase and can be provided a higher weightage.

14.5   Patents

In research institutes of India, patents automatically belong to institutes (eg. IIT). Why? The logic behind this is not clear. Despite the fact that the institutes claim that patents belong to the institute, the institute cannot file the patent without consent of the faculty inventor.

So, why does the faculty meekly surrender their rights so easily? Whom does it benefit? One reason for this meek surrender is the high cost of filing the patent and maintaining it. In fact, patent allows filing **provisional patent application**. This helps the inventor protect his intellectual rights while he experiments and collaborates with others. In these institutes, the cost factor disallows such things. As a result, often there is a conflict of who the original inventor is – the student or the faculty.

The worst thing is that such patents rarely brings in income to the institute. Leaving aside exceptional cases, most of the patents are filed for prestige or promotion purpose. In fact, the institutes suffer huge financial burden to maintain these patents

14.6   Private Investment in Research and Development

Investments in R&D from private companies are exempt of service tax. There are two parts of such investments

a)   Instrument, consumable and salary to staff and students

b)   Honorarium to faculty

Often, it is the later that is important to drive the research. However, most institute rules are such that it is difficult to pay this and there is no overall profit to the company in investing in R&D activities. As a result, the proportion of investment that comes from private companies in R&D remains negligible. Following suggestions are proposed:

a)   **New/Replacement Equipment Fund**: In place of expecting complete instrument to come from an individual work, instrument fund can be created where small quantum of money can come from each work. For example, a UTM (Universal Testing Machine) costs about 2 crores. To expect payment from an individual source is difficult. For on purchase of an equipment like this, a fund for its replacement may be created. All consultancy and research work carried out using this machine should pay a small amount on this replacement fund. This machine must have been purchase in 1960s and if this fund had been created earlier, there would be no problem in replacing this equipment.

b) **No limitation on faculty honorarium** percentage be implemented. If the equipment exists, payment would be expected in new/replacement equipment fund. Institute may take its own component of share. Forcing expenses on equipment when it is not required makes the investment financially non-viable.

14.7 Right to participate in Politics

Researchers and scientists have a very fertile brain. They have been advisor to the government all throughout the history. In Germany and few other places educated people are starting to take active interest in politics. Let us look at the following few cases:

1. **Chanakya Kautilya**[1]: He was originally a professor of economics and political science at the ancient university of Taxila. He has authored the book "Arthasastra" (Economics) and is considered as the pioneer of political science and classical economics. On the other hand, he assisted Mauryan emperor Chandragupta to rise to power which is the first empire in India to have archeologically recorded history. He served as a chief advisor to both Chandragupta and his son Bindusara.

2. **Angela Dorothea Merkel**, is one of the most respected politician in Europe. She started her political career in divided East Germany finally became the chancellor of Germany in 2005. Today, she is considered as the voice of the European Union and is able to impact major decisions in the world today. But to start with, she studied physics at the University of Leipzig, earning a doctorate in 1978, and later worked as a chemist at the Central Institute for Physical Chemistry, Academy of Sciences (1978–90).

....Like most young people in the German Democratic Republic (East Germany), Merkel was a member of the Free German Youth (FDJ), the official youth movement sponsored by the ruling Socialist Unity Party. Although membership was nominally voluntary, those who did not join found it all but impossible to be admitted to higher education. [2]

This means, people in higher education in East Germany was almost forced to participate in the Government. This is the story of one of the most powerful highly educated leader of a country. She holds the highest degree, and her husband is also a quantum chemist and professor.

3. **Johanna Wanka** [3] is the Federal Minister of Education and Research in German Ministry. She attended the Polytechnic Secondary School in Großtreben and the advanced school in Torgau before studying mathematics at Leipzig University in the GDR. From 1974 on, she was a research assistant at Merseburg University of Applied Sciences, where she received her doctorate in 1980. In 1993 she became professor of engineering mathematics at Merseburg University of Applied Sciences. In March 1994, she was elected rector of that university, a position she retained until taking office as minister in October 2000.

In India, the faculty members of government colleges are officially Government servant. There is a rule that Government servant cannot participate in the political process of forming a government, as they are privy to information that runs the government. The following News Paper clipping on September 22, 2010 explains the mater nicely:

The Madras High Court bench here has held that government employees could be prohibited from being members of political parties and it would not amount to denying their fundamental rights.

Dismissing a writ petition by an employee of Civil Supplies Department Justice S Nagamuthu said "such prohibition will come under the purview of reasonable restrictions imposed on the fundamental rights."

Though a person could not be denied entry into government service on the sole ground that he was involved in active politics, he could not be allowed to continue it after taking up government jobs as it would not be in the interest of discipline or proper discharge of duties attached to the service.

"If any employee chooses to serve the nation by being a member of a political party, he can do so without continuing as a government servant. If he chooses to serve the nation as a government servant then he should forego his involvement in politics," the judge said.

This rule is extended and applied to the faculty members, as they also receive salary from Government of India. Unlike the actual officers involved in daily running of the government, the faculty members do not have any role in the government. Will not the government and the people of India be benefitted by their active participation? The following are the possible way a faculty member can logically contribute to the country:

a) One problem that is anticipated is disturbance of the educational scenario when active politics are allowed inside the educational institute. Recent ban of a political group in IIT Madras has ignited this debate. Authors feel that public demonstration, disturbing the educational atmosphere should be discouraged. Rules should be setup for such activity to be held in non-working/class hours so that normal activities are not hampered.

b) Faculty members should be allowed to visit political parties in their spare time and allowed to act as advisor, as long as their own activity is not effected. This will allow them to test how much the system need them, possibility of contribution, necessity of active participation, interest and future scope before taking up active politics. They should also be allowed to be member of any political party as they choose.

c) Even when active participation in politics is necessary, for the greater interest of the individual and country, the possibility of participation in academic as a part time faculty can be allowed.

d) The role in active politics may often be temporary for 5-10 years. Hence, the faculty should be allowed to join back the educational institute, when they agree to quit political life.

For any country, it is important that each and every section of the population be allowed to participate and influence the government. Disallowing the most educated section of the society to not participate in such an important activity does not benefit anyone. For a young faculty, asking him to leave the job if he wishes to join politics is not a logical thing and the price he is being asked to pay to serve in this uncertain world of politics is too high. Are the film artist and sportsman asked to stop their activity when then join politics?

The world would be a better place if the brightest and most intelligent people of the world become leaders. In most countries, the faculty members of the university shy away from politics. How can we say that the government by the people, when the most educated and intelligent lot are not even allowed to participate in the party politics? Should we not reconsider this mater of fundamental right of a faculty member to participate in running the government a little more sincerely? Would India not benefit by their participation? Allowing them to participate in a flexible manner would surely benefit this world.

14.8　Conclusion

Indian Government should try to make the research atmosphere better by seriously looking into the following points:

a)　Implement National Conference system

b)　Formulate Effective Patent policy

c)　Provide honorarium to faculty undertaking projects

d)　Provide incentive to Private Bodies to invest in R&D activities

e)　Create transparency and public participation in research

f)　Allow Faculty members to participate in active politics in a logical way.

References

1.　https://en.wikipedia.org/wiki/Chanakya
2.　https://en.wikipedia.org/wiki/Angela_Merkel
3.　https://en.wikipedia.org/wiki/Johanna_Wanka
4.　http://www.thehindu.com/news/cities/Madurai/employees-prohibited-to-join-political-parties-asserts-hc/article776955.ece (24/6/2015).

EPILOGUE

This book is just a start of a journey, which has multiple-destinations; it is a beginning of an endless quest for making qualitative differences in lives of masses, by adopting some new creative ideas, approach and attitudes and evolving them into implementable projects. This book is written primarily to address the plight of children suffering from the present education system and touch upon their physical and mental growth and other related issues.

Authors would take this opportunity to express their sincere thanks and regards, from the bottom of the heart to the readers, who has now, became part of this movement of change. We expect all to be change-agents, to lead the world to a bright future. Our intention is to create a wave, which could be carried to the far-ending shores of the continents. We request the readers to discuss and share these concepts with their friends, families and colleagues in all possible forums and social media groups. They might disagree on some issues, but a healthy debates followed by little action will change many things. They are also requested to send us their views through our website or emails and become proactive in making local groups/clubs/forums for engaging and initiating discussions with government, social organisations and educational groups.

Authors would also like to express gratitude to the governmental agencies, which have read the book and granted us time to interact and give valuable feedback. It is only through the support of the policy makers and administrators, that we can change the attitudes of the society and institutions, for making India a progressive and developed country. Just following the old and outdated educational, sports and research systems, without positively questioning them, will not change the pathetic situations prevailing. Government policy makers and implementing agencies are requested to create independent research group to investigate possibilities of discussion and implementation of these concepts.

Since, this book is circulated worldwide, it is expected that it will initiate similar conceptual and action-oriented movements in many countries. It would be better if these efforts are carried out with international committee, so that experts all over the world can exchange their views. India is a growing economy and it would be good if we become humble and try to understand that how many of the countries had already started their journey in similar lines long back. It is better to learn the lessons and build upon the momentum of development.

We have much expectation from the International and Multinational Developmental agencies like United Nations, UNICEF, WHO, Olympic association and other agencies including the Embassies. It will be aiming to make all these organization aware of the new and innovative ideas, which can be integrated in the various developmental projects in India. Support and more guidance are expected from these agencies, which can also help us in initiating some pilot projects to build different change modules in education sports and research field.

Media, in 21st century has become the most important opinion-makers. We will engage the print, electronic and social media in this movement and with their support make a significant impact on the development and growth of society and system. We welcome media to fulfil their social and moral obligations, by joining us in this great cause of nation's building.

We also expect the companies, industry groups, the CSR organisations and other private entrepreneurs to join us in making some positive changes. They can support is in many ways financially as well as morally.

The Non- Governmental organisations and other Civic Society organisation have to play a prominent role in realising our dream to develop our children as a valuable assets of national development. These social organisations will be leading this battle from the front, with pro-active participation of their volunteers and social workers. They will be become our most valuable partners in heralding a great change in the attitudes and behaviours of the people and the state machinery.

We would also like to request the government to allow the originator of this movement, Dr. Gupta to participate in these efforts, in any possible way. Currently, being a government servant in IIT Delhi, he is not allowed by the service rules to participate in the activities to guide others and get paid for his contribution. His inability to officially participate is hampering the activities of the group. He loves teaching and being with the growing youth, as he teaches them the ways of life; trying to change a few drops in the ocean along with the professional subjects. In fact, Dr. Gupta fails to understand why Government of India is not willing to take service of the most intellectual people of the country – IIT faculty, in such social causes officially. In case he get paid for his contribution, he would not mind sharing the income with his institution as per rules.

This group led by Dr. Gupta faces an uphill task. The work is being initiated by making an official website, where people will be able to read and follow the activities of our group with transparency. Dr. Gupta is the face of this mass movement and his presence is strongly required, so a formal permission from Human Resources Ministry is much needed. All efforts will be taken to legalize his participation in this movement and public support is sought in this matter.

The group is planning a national and international study-tour, covering as many countries from Russia to UK, with an objective to be able to interact with people and presenting the concepts with government and non-government bodies. The aim is to initiate actions so that international movement and action groups could be created to discuss and implement projects, for bringing changes in the society. In this trip, Dr. Gupta plans the following activities:

1. Workshops to explain the concepts presented in the book.
2. Understand the status of sports, exercise, music, and dance and sports science in India in comparison to that abroad.

3. To explore the possible partnership in sports coaching between Indian and reputed sports training centres in other country.

4. To explore the possible partnership in sports science between Indian Universities and reputed sports universities other country and explore the possible scholarship for Indian students these colleges abroad.

5. Explore possibility of incorporation of a private (people) driven research culture special in social fields.

6. Explore possibility of sports and educational portal.

7. Initiate studies on comparative life of women from across the world.

8. Creating of technical teams of doctor, psychologists, physiotherapists and nutritionists to support all the children pursuing sports.

The group invites all people who think they can contribute in any manner – financially, logistically, technical website support, support as expert in the field, initiate research in educational and non-educational world, initiating debate, organizing lecture in a financially viable way.

Comments from Reader

Since 2003, we have seen Dr. Gupta diving into various issues in a calculated manner, making us do deep introspection. Often his ideas are misunderstood, but he always took criticism with open heart, positive attitude and sincerity. We have also seen him facing various crises of life like a cool yogi. We all stood beside him. Practically, we were witness to this journey as the book was being written.

Author's genuine concern for the problems faced by the teenagers, women and old people in India is reflected honestly and some very bold solutions are proposed. The record of his own experiments with truth indicates his considerable integrity and courage.

This book takes one through the entire life cycle of an individual; it shatters lots of myths and stereotypes, pointing the fundamental flaws in the way we deal with the things in life. Simply brilliant!

Dr. Gurmail Benipal and **Dr. K. Ramachandra Rao**,
Faculty IIT Delhi

This book is like a bundle of knowledge about child care & education system and is an eye-opener for all. This touches the life of a woman as a mother, a wife and a career person. The keyword of this journey is a pragmatic balanced stand between flexible education, healthy body and personal development. This will benefit all sections of the society. Being a mother and a homemaker, I strongly feel that the child rearing practices of Japan (Hoikuen) should be introduced in our country to liberate the women and allow them to work without worrying.

The book has also beautifully explained the specific psychological goals of people crossing different stages of their lives, explaining the importance of counselling at every stage. The book is a pleasure to read and has a great potential to change the world for our children in a positive way. This will make our children physically and mentally strong to enjoy their life with clearly defined aims and objectives. I would be happy to be part of the social change movement inducted by the concepts sowed here.

Jayeeta Dasgupta, New Delhi
Homemaker, Mother of two Children.

I am a teacher and quite good in Maths and Science subjects. But my son had serious difficulty in Maths. We had to even change his school due to this Maths-phobia. Finally, he marginally passed class X. In class XI, he choose Commerce and as the pressure of Maths decreased, he blossomed and flourished. Today he is a successful lawyer. If my son had failed to clear class X due to Maths, his academic life would had been totally destroyed.

I strongly support the idea of bifurcation of streams after class VIII. A large number of students will surely be benefitted, as they do not require the sophisticated level of maths and science as taught in class IX and X. This will also allow the students more enjoyable study and relaxed and fruitful life. The proposal of an independent Entertainment Stream for children opting for sports, music and dance is a great concept. To start with, the entertainment stream may be provided as an option after class VIII with possibilities of sports, music, dance, multi-media, etc. as strong interconnected options.

An Optimistic Parent

I and my wife read this book together. It was completely a new experience reading it. It took us unusually long time to complete as we always got stuck in each chapter as we invariably started discussion on the topics. After reading the book, we met the authors and decided to start discussion groups among our friends. We realized it is important to face the truth to create a better world for our children and us.

Nitin Chaurasia
Technical Superintendent, IIT Delhi

Appeal

This book symbolizes the hope of the Authors to make positive contribution in the lives of people around the world with an action-based innovative approach. The purpose is to make qualitative positive changes in their lives, with the active participation of like-minded people, who want to join, support or contribute in any form. We also seek active support from Individuals, NGOs and Government agencies worldwide.

You can invite even Dr. Gupta for lectures and workshops. All willing to participate in this movement or to contribute financially are requested to contact through details provided in the contact list. You will get status update in the website, twitter and Facebook. Small drops of support will create a Tsunami wave of positive changes in the Society.

Contact

Author: Dr. Supratic Gupta
Designation: Faculty, IIT Delhi
Mobile: +91-8860794422
Address: Civil Engineering Dept.,
IIT Delhi, Hauz Khas,
New Delhi-110016
Email: supratic68@gmail.com

Co-Author: Mr. Prakash Chandra
Designation: NGO Consultant,
Life Coach/Counsellor,
Research Assistant,
Mind Valley Consulting Pvt. Ltd.
Email: prakchandra008@gmail.com

Email: supratic.prakash@gmail.com

Printed in the United States
By Bookmasters